FIFTY *Soviet* POETS

**Compiled by Vladimir Ognev
and Dorian Rottenberg**

**Fredonia Books
Amsterdam, The Netherlands**

Fifty Soviet Poets

Compiled by
Vladimir Ognev
Dorian Rottenberg

ISBN: 1-58963-604-X

Reprinted from the 1974 edition

Fredonia Books
Amsterdam, the Netherlands
http://www.fredoniabooks.com

CONTENTS

7

9

Introduction

Considering the almost universal loss of interest in
poetry, observable in this age of scientific progress,
the growing demand for books of verse in the Soviet
Union appears as a somewhat unusual phenomenon.
But there are many historical and social reasons
to account for the popularity of Soviet poetry.

The historical reason is the birth of our new society
which opened such wonderful prospects before each
individual and mankind as a whole. Soviet art was
launched amid an unprecedented upsurge of creative
energy and, as Mayakovsky said, poetry received
such an enormous charge of this energy from the Rev-
olution that "millions of hearts were set in mo-
tion".

Now for the social and more up-to-date reasons.
Two diametrically opposite viewpoints have clashed
in mid-twentieth-century literature: one preaches
faith in the power of reason, and in the ability of
Man to control the elemental forces of matter which
he himself has unleashed; the other predicts a global
calamity, shows an utter lack of faith in Man's creat-
ive power, a passive acquiescence to the individual's
"withdrawal" and "isolation", and the general dis-
integration of human links. Hamlet's words "The
time is out of joint" are taken as an absolute fact,
with complete disregard for what he says next: "O
cursed spite, that ever I was born to set it right."

But poetry means hope. And when hope has a solid,
tangible basis, and the people's confidence in them-
selves is further bolstered up by the romance of poetry,
then a precious spark of mutual understanding be-
tween poet and reader is kindled. In poetry the reader
will find support for his faith in such human virtues
as dignity, fortitude and loyalty.

In this collection we have included the works of
fifty poets differing in style and belonging to different

generations, published in the last ten years. We selected these poems with a view to demonstrating the great diversity and range of themes in Soviet art and the uniqueness of our poets' creative personalities (as far as this can be rendered in translation). The wealth of Soviet poetry is not, of course, exhausted by the present collection. We were somewhat restricted in our choice because it had to be translatable poetry and preferably poetry that did not call for any additional explanatory notes. Even so, we believe that some of the best that Soviet poetry has produced in the last ten years has been included here.

We also hope that by giving a parallel text in Russian we shall be helping those readers who possess some knowledge of the language to gain a better understanding of the original. In this collection we offer the reader verses by national poets translated into Russian by leading Russian poets.

This volume contains poetry by writers of the older generation who have become our classics—Anna Akhmatova and Boris Pasternak; poets of the 1950's—Nikolai Zabolotsky and Leonid Martynov; lyrics of the middle generation—Boris Slutsky, Rasul Gamzatov, Yevgeni Vinokurov, Kaisyn Kuliev and Eduardas Mieželaitis; and the brilliant galaxy of young talent—Andrei Voznesensky, Yevgeni Yevtushenko and Bella Akhmadulina.

The reader will climb up the steps of this poetic ladder into a house that is strange to him but which, we are sure, he will find peopled with understandable problems, passions and dreams. He will find a world of lofty emotions, of patriotism and high ideals, which at the same time is a world of psychological and emotional secrets (Anna Akhmatova), of complex emotional processes (Boris Pasternak), of exacting moral self-examination (Smelyakov, Tvardovsky), of a subtle awareness of beauty (Chikovani, Bella Akhmadulina), of apprehension and stress (Martynov, Voznesensky), of fairy-tale magic (Svetlov), of defiance against all that is outworn and obsolete (Yevtushenko, Drach, Vācietis).

In some of the poems the reader will encounter the commonplaces of life, the unsophisticated language of the street, and a certain crudity of subject matter—such is the poetry of Boris Slutsky, in others—in the lyricism of Vinokurov and in the melancholy meditations of the Jewish poet Galkin—he will find a gracefully logical construction and a subtle communication of thought.

The villagers' idiom, simple yet shrewd and wise, of the Daghestan poet Rasul Gamzatov makes a striking contrast to the intricate imaginativeness of the language employed by Semyon Kirsanov who continues in the steps of that great experimenter Mayakovsky.

At the outset Soviet poetry abounded in trends or "schools", such as the "Smithy", "Komsomol Group", LEF's, Constructivists, and others. Selvinsky and Lugovskoy, for instance, originally belonged to the constructivist school, but all that has remained in their writing of the principles proclaimed by this school—formal strictness of composition, contempt for "shapeless" feelings, preaching of cool-headed calculation and expediency—is perhaps their craftsmanship and their excellent handling of form. The credo of the LEF's (the Left Front of Art) has also undergone a change. Still, such slogans of the "leftists" as emphasis on fact and focus on topical problems have been an influence on a par with many others and also remained the basic principles in the art of Aseyev and Kirsanov, the chief exponents of the LEF programme.

Modern Soviet poetry has absorbed the finest traditions of those schools, popular in the 1920s, as evidenced by the work of our younger poets. Invisible but very strong ties exist between Yevtushenko and Mayakovsky, and between Voznesensky and both Pasternak and Marina Tsvetayeva. Many of the younger poets like to feel that they are the direct descendants of the Russian avant-garde poets of the 1920s. The older generation, on the other hand, who began with formal experiments arrived, towards the end of their careers, at the wisdom of simple form and thus established a certain degree of continuity with the 19th-century classics. This is not a paradox. In the development of poetry, innovation and tradition are indissoluble. A fresh upsurge in innovation usually means that a new quality has ripened in poetry.

In modern Soviet poetry, the accent on ideology, which has always been its distinguishing feature, remains as strong as ever except that now it is woven into the fabric of the imagery itself. The reason for this change is that the readers themselves have changed. They have gained historical experience and have attained a higher cultural level and acquired greater discernment. Their interest in psychological poetry has grown tremendously. Russian literature, of course, has always been famous for its probings into the innermost recesses of the individual's soul. Once Alexander Blok quite rightly stated that at a time of historical storms and alarms, the most intimate recesses of the soul are also filled with alarm. Vladimir Mayakovsky, the greatest poet of the Revolution, wrote: "That's how it was with the soldiers, or perhaps with the country, or maybe that's how it was in my heart." This indivisibility of the macroworld of ideas and the microworld of emotions, this merging of the interests of society with the individual's private interests is reflected in our art not as mere declarations but as the norm in our way of life.

This explains why in the poetry of the 1950s and 1960s we find such an increasing variety of genres, styles and idioms. After all, there are as many different ways of striving for a common goal as there are individualities.

The idea of the revolutionary transformation of life, of heroism in the name of the people, runs through the whole of Soviet art. Without losing this "Promethean" quality Soviet poetry has become more humane, so to speak, in the past ten years. Humanism cannot be examined in isolation from its moral foundations: characteristically this book ends with two poems about goodness and integrity by Alexander Yashin. These virtues are inherent in Soviet poetry, the roots of which are national but whose aspirations are common to all mankind, and they are a guarantee of its viability. Poetry such as this will find a response in people everywhere. It carries a message of brotherhood and challenges violence and enmity. It stands up for the world's simple and eternal values: free labour, motherhood, creativity, the joy of communion with Nature, and friendship between all peoples.

Vladimir OGNEV

Irakli Abashidze (b. 1909) is one of the leading modern poets of Soviet Georgia. He was educated at Tbilisi University and brought out his verse in print for the first time in 1928. The optimistic, resolute rhythms of his poetry of the 1930s ("New Poems", 1938) gave way to heroic solemnity in the pre-war and war years. The crowning achievement of Abashidze's art is to be found in the cycle "Shota Rustaveli" and its sequel "Palestine, Palestine" written in the 1960s. The poet, speaking in the name of Rustaveli, begins his confession at the walls of the Monastery of the Holy Cross in Palestine where, according to legend, the great Georgian poet and enlightener died. It is as though the voice of the ancient poet is brought back from the dead. It can be heard in the monastery, in the olive grove, in the white monastery cell, and on the shore of the Dead Sea. It speaks to us across the ages about love, loyalty, patriotism and hope.

IRAKLI ABASHIDZE

ИРАКЛИЙ АБАШИДЗЕ

Поэтам Индии

Не хочу враждовать
Я ни с кем в этом мире.
Но хочу побывать
На большом мушаири.

Кровь пока не стара,
Сердце бьётся, как птица
Я хочу у костра
С вами песней сразиться.

Чтоб в словах огневых
Было больше накала,
Чтоб услышали их
Возле стен Тадж-Магала,

Чтобы круг был не тесен
При луне до рассвета...
На сражение песен
Выводите поэтов!

Мы на вашей земле
Нашу бурку расстелем,
В лунной сказочной мгле
Стрелы песен нацелим.

Оживут наши думы
От сердечного жара,

To the Poets of India

I wish nobody woe
On this planet, war-weary,
What I wish is to go
To a World Mushairi*

Where, lit up by a fire,
Bards and singers would throng,
And the night would go by
In a contest of song.

Whose resonant words
Would arouse Taj-Mahal
And circle the world
While the moonbeams fall.

For a battle of verse
Rally, bards of the earth
And let none feel the worse
On displaying his worth.

We shall spread on your ground
Our Caucasian burka**
And our ballads will sound
For both Indian and Gurkha.

Let our songs ring afar
With the warmth of our hearts;

* Mushairi—Oriental poetry festival.
** Sheepskin mantle worn by Caucasian highlanders

Выводите Махмуда,
Выводите Сардара!

Никому не грозя,
Стрелы скрестятся в выси.
Выводите, друзья,
В бой Ахмада Фаизи.

Через лунную мглу
Жарким солнечным словом
Вместе грянем хвалу
Вашей Индии новой.

Воспоем красоту
Ваших девушек милых
И волшебницу ту,
Что меня опьянила.

Дружбой сердце согрев,
Для Тбилиси и Дели
Грянет хинди напев
И язык Руставели...

Не хочу воевать
Я ни с кем в этом мире,
Лишь хочу побывать
На большом мушаири.

Come, Mahmood and Sardar,
To our battle of arts.

We will rouse no man's fear
Crossing arms in the night.
Come, my friends, gather near,
Let Faiz join the fight!

While the moon pours its rays,
Evanescent and weightless,
Flaming words will sing praise
To new India's greatness.

We shall sing of the charms
Of the Indian maid
And the velvety arms
That my fancy invade.

Kindling friendship in souls
From Tbilisi and Delhi,
Hindi verses will blend
With the rhythms of Khartveli

I wish nobody woe
On this planet, war-weary.
All I wish is to go
To a World Mushairi!

Translated by Dorian Rottenberg

Margarita Aligher (b. 1915) is a Russian poetess. She began to write poetry in 1933, from 1934 to 1937 she studied at the Gorky Institute of Literature. Fame came to her with "Zoya" (1942)—a tragic story of the Moscow schoolgirl Zoya Kosmodemyanskaya and her heroic death in the Great Patriotic War of 1941-1945. This work is written in the form of a direct address to the readers. In her poems "Your Victory" (1945), "Beautiful Mecha" (1951) and her poetry of the last ten years, Margarita Aligher continues to develop the main theme of her art—the need for complete honesty in human relations, heroic self-sacrifice, understanding, and moral uprightness. Her poetry throbs like a taut wire, and her choice of words is usually of a conversational variety.

MARGARITA ALIGHER

МАРГАРИТА АЛИГЕР

Просека

Есть в моем лесу одна дорога,
где
   с утра,
      в ночи,
           на склоне дня
Кто-то смотрит пристально и строго
Сквозь прямые сосны на меня.
Глаз не отводя и не мигая,
Кто-то смотрит на меня в упор:

— Я-то думал, ты теперь другая,
Ну а ты,
все та же ты,
с тех пор...
Так же все и маешься?
А я-то...
Я-то думал... Я-то был бы рад...

Повожу плечами виновато
и навстречу поднимаю взгляд.
Вижу высоко над головою
сосны, облака, голубизну,
хлопья снега, вековую хвою,
лето, осень, зиму и весну.
Вспоминаю жизнь свою с начала
и невольно замедляю шаг...

My Path

In my forest there's a path where always,
Be it morning,
                    afternoon,
                                    or night,
Someone looks at me attentively and closely
Through the wall of slender, stately pines.
Someone always watches me, unblinking,
With a stare that's piercing and intent:

"You'd have altered greatly, I was thinking
You're the same,
You haven't changed since then.
Still unhappy?
Somehow I expected...
I'd be glad if it were otherwise..."

With a shrug and smile apologetic
I look up to face those watchful eyes.
And I see high overhead above me
Treetops,
            clouds,
                        the azure skies...
Winter, springtime, summer, autumn...
Flakes of snow,
                    and ageless pines...
I recall my life from the beginning,
And I pause my heart to search.

Что успела?

        Все не так да мало.

Что свершила?

           Мало да не так.

Все-то я живу уж как умею.

Много ли умею, вот вопрос?!

Все-то я надеюсь, что успею.

Как бы после плакать не пришлось.

Не пришлось бы спохватиться поздно

Все ли впрямь задачи решены?

Кто-то смотрит ласково и грозно

С тихой неприступной вышины.

Есть в моем лесу одна дорога,

Просека,

        пробитый в чаще путь...

И шепчу я:

        — Подожди немного!

Я счастливой стану как-нибудь.

Я осилю — обещаю свято —

мелкий вздор, неправду и вражду...

И в ответ я слышу:

        — Ладно, я-то...

Я-то верю... Я-то подожду...

Я-то что... Вот ты-то как?

        — Не знаю...

— Постарайся все-таки дойти...

Жизнь моя — дорога та лесная,

неизменный свет в конце пути.

What have I accomplished?
                    Nothing, really.
What have I created?
                    Nothing much.
Always I am struggling on as best I can.
Is my best enough, though, when all's said and done?
I am always hoping that there's lots of time.
Will I not be sorry when I find there's none?

Won't it be too late for me to realise
That I had more problems still to fight.

Someone's watching me with sternly gentle eyes
From those unassailable and quiet heights.

In my forest there's a certain road which I...
It's a clearing wrested from the thickets.
"I'll be happier,
                    just give me one more try.
I will somehow manage yet."
                                    I whisper.
"I'll get over everything, I swear.
All those petty hurts,
                    and lies,
                            and hate..."

And I hear in answer: "Fair is fair.
I believe you. You will try. I'll wait.
Are you sure yourself?"
                    —"I do not know."—
"Still, do try to make it, don't succumb."

All my life, along that forest path I'll go,
Following a, light that bids me come...

Translated by Olga Shartse

Двое

Опять они поссорились в трамвае,
не сдерживаясь, не стыдясь чужих...
Но зависти невольной не скрывая,
взволнованно глядела я на них.

Они не знают, как они счастливы.
И слава богу! Ни к чему им знать.
Подумать только! — рядом, оба живы
и можно все исправить и понять.

The Lucky Two

They had a quarrel in the tram again.
Oblivious of the crowd, they let off steam.
But I, I frankly envied them
As, deeply stirred, I watched the scene.

It's best that they have no misgivings
And do not know how fortunate they are.
To think that both of them are living
And can still work their troubles out!

Translated by Olga Shartse

«ДА» и «НЕТ»

Если было б мне теперь
восемнадцать лет,
я охотнее всего
отвечала б: нет!

Если было б мне теперь
года двадцать два,
я охотнее всего
отвечала б: да!

Но для прожитых годов.
пережитых лет,
мало этих малых слов,
этих «да» и «нет».

Мою душу рассказать
им не по плечу.
Не расспрашивай меня,
если я молчу.

Yes and No

Were I in my teens again,
Seventeen or so,
My most ready answer then
Would, I'm sure, be: no.

Now, if I were twenty-two
I can safely guess
That my quickest answer would
Be most surely: yes.

They're inadequate, those two
Little "yes" and "no",
After what I have lived through
Since that long ago.

All my feelings to express
They would be too weak.
So don't ask me, do not press,
If I do not speak.

Translated by Olga Shartse

Pavel Antokolsky, the son of a St. Petersburg lawyer, was born in 1896. He studied at the Law Faculty of Moscow University. Later he worked at the Vakhtangov Theatre in Moscow as an actor and then a producer. His first book of verse came out in 1922. The collections "West" (1926), "Third Book" (1927), "Robespiere and the Gorgon" (1928) and the poem "François Villon" (1934) belong to the romantic period of his work, dedicated mainly to history. Antokolsky lost his only son in the Great Patriotic War, and to him he dedicated his famous poem "Son" (1943)—a philosophical, publicistic requiem commemorating the generation which fell in battle against nazism. The last ten years Antokolsky has written a great deal. His emotional and intellectual poetry is analytical in character. A highly cultured man, Antokolsky has the acumen of a critic and the intuition of a pedagogue. He is known as a skilful translator from French, Bulgarian and several languages of the peoples of the U.S.S.R.

PAVEL ANTOKOLSKY

ПАВЕЛ АНТОКОЛЬСКИЙ

Действующие лица говорят

Что ты нам сказало?
Что нам приказало?
Зачем в темноту театрального зала
Ты, время, ударило прожекторами?
Мы сами участвуем в собственной

драме.

Мы сами ее начинаем.
Но завтра
Не кончим, —
Пускай приготовится автор!

Молчишь?
Ты достаточно долго молчало.
Куда же ты мчишь?
Начинайся сначала!
Все прошлые дни и года возврати нам.
Довольно ты числишься необратимым,
Ломаешь чертоги,
Едва возведешь их,
Стираешь итоги,
Едва подведешь их!

Нам мало одной только жизни прекрасной,
Опасной и страстной,
Хотя и напрасно!
Нам мало, что собственной жизненной

жаждой

Посмертно реабилитирован каждый!

The *Dramatis Personae* Have Their Say

What advice did you accord us?
What directions afford us?
Why, into the darkness of the auditorium
Have you, Time, released your blinding footlights?
We are actors in our own play, not playwrights.
The drama is ours. We begin it.
But not ours
To finish—
The sequel is up to the author!

Struck dumb?
Come, enough of your silent spinning.
Why press on and on?
Go back to the beginning!
All our past days and years—we claim the lot
                                    back
Long enough we believed: one can't put the clock
                                    back
Even as you create,
You destroy, all-engulfing.
Though you leave a clean slate
You add up to nothing!

It is not enough—our one brief, beautiful life
Walking the edge of the knife
In pointless passion and strife.
Not enough that each vital individual is fated
To be posthumously rehabilitated!

Нам мало,
Что ты черепа нам ломало
И вновь поднимало!
Нам этого мало!

Зажги нам глаза миллионами молний
И клетки грудные озоном наполни,
И в ноздри ударь резедой и левкоем!
Одним только не награждай нас — покоем
Но всей невесомой твоей каруселью
Верни нашу молодость на повоселье!

Так будет —
О, только бы часа дождаться!
Так будет —
Иначе не стоит рождаться!
Так будет,
И это пребудет вовеки
Биением пульса в любом человеке.
Он старую тяжбу со смертью рассудит
И мертвых разбудит.

В р е м я:
            Так будет. Т а к б у д е т.

Not enough
That, having broken our skulls, you must
Raise us up anew from earth and dust!
It is not enough!

Light a million lightnings to flame in our eyeballs,
Blast sweet-stock and reseda into our nostrils,
Expand with ozone our heaving breast,
One gift only withholding—rest!
And, as your aerial roundabout comes full circle
Give us back our youth with our life's revival.

And so it shall be.
Ah, would I might see that day dawn,
So it shall be.
To what other end were we born?
For so it shall be
And so shall abide for all of us
Beating on in the pulse of every man Jack of us
Abrogating Mortality's ancient edict
Breaking Death's secret...

Time
So be it! SO BE IT!

Translated by Avril Pyman

Я убеждаюсь непрестанно

Я убеждаюсь непрестанно,
Что мир еще загадок полн:
Изгибом девичьего стана,
Сверканьем молний, пляской волн.

Но безрассудно и бесплодно
Сжигаю честный черновик
За то, что к трезвости холодной
Он недостаточно привык.

Что ж, значит, дальше не поедем.
Разорван беглый наш союз.
С тетрадью, как цыган с медведем
Я на распутье остаюсь.

Искусство сделано из глины,
Гаданья, гибели, огня.
Я данник этой дисциплины,
Не осуждайте же меня!

My Conviction

It's my conviction, mounting ever,
That Earth is yet a wondrous place;
There's high romance in stormy weather,
In dancing waves, in maiden grace.

But in a feckless, fruitless fashion
My first impressions I condemn
For lack of sober, cold dispassion,
And feed my notebooks to the flame.

Our ways no longer lie together
Our short-lived partnership ends here
And lightly I throw my rough notes over
And turn a new page, void and clear.

The elements of art are clay,
Calamity, witch-craft, ardour.
Then judge me not for, come what may,
Art is my Alma Mater!

Translated by Avril Pyman

*Nikolai Aseyev (1889-1963)—was a true follower of
Mayakovsky in his bold experimenting, a man who was
in love with the Russian language and Russian history.
He was a lyric poet "by the very pattern of his soul"
as he himself used to say. His melodious poetry is
intuitive and spontaneous in character, and his
rhythms are vigorous, clear-cut and ingenious. Till the
end of his days Aseyev would turn again and again
to the themes of the turbulent unforgettable days of
his youth. He earned his greatest popularity with
his poem "Mayakovsky Begins" (1940), the collec-
tions "Meditations" (1955) and "Attunement"
(1961). These collections contain his philosophical
reflections on the destiny of man in history.*

NIKOLAI ASEYEV

НИКОЛАЙ АСЕЕВ

Еще за деньги люди держатся

Еще за деньги
                    люди держатся,
как за кресты
                    держались люди
во времена
                    глухого Керженца,
но вечно этого не будет.
Еще за властью
                    люди тянутся,
не зная меры
                    и цены ей,
но долго
            это не останется —
настанут времена иные.
Еще гоняются
                    за славою, —
охотников до ней
                    несметно, —
стараясь
            хоть бы тенью слабою
остаться на земле
                    посмертно.
Мне кажется,
                что власть и почести —
вода соленая
                    морская:
чем дольше пить,
                    тем больше хочется
а жажда
            все не отпускает.

There Are Some
Folk Who Money Covet

There are some folk
                who money covet,
as heathens
            idols, long ago,
they cannot
            get sufficient of it,
but this will not be always so.
There are some folk
                who crave for power
who know no curbs,
              nor ken its worth,
but soon will come their final hour,
and other times will come to earth.
There are some folk
                pursuing glory,
it seems
        that legion is their name,
their only hope,
              that in some story
their names
            for ever will remain.
It seems
        that power and adulation,
are really
           very much like brine:
You drink and drink
              without cessation,
and still you're thirsty
                all the time.

И личное твое
                            бессмертие
не в том,
              что кто ты,
                              как ты,
                                         где ты, —
а всех земных племен
                            соцветие,
созвездие
          людей планеты!
С тех пор
          как шар земной наш кружится,
сквозь вечность
                        продолжая мчаться,
великое
          людей содружество
впервые
          стало намечаться.
Чтоб все — и белые,
                          и черные,
и желтые
          земного братства —
вошли в широкие,
                        просторные
края
    всеобщего богатства.

Your own,
         your private
                        immortality
is not
     in station,
                rank or birth:
your this, your that—
                   what triviality—
it's in the future
                of your earth!
And since
         the earth began its spinning,
since man
         upon his feet first stood,
we see at last,
             the faint beginning
of universal
           brotherhood.
May every
         colour
              be invited,
to share
       the world's
                 abundant good,
to come together,
               live united,
as decent human beings should.

Translated by Eugene Felgenhauer

Соловей

Вот опять
соловей
со своей
стародавнею песнею...
Ей пора бы давно уж
на пенсию!

Да и сам соловей
инвалид...
Отчего ж —
лишь осыплет руладами
волоса
холодок шевелит
и становятся души
крылатыми!

Песне тысячи лет,
а нова:
будто только что
полночью сложена;
от нее
и луна,
и трава,
и деревья
стоят заворожено.

Песне — тысячи лет,
а жива:
с нею вольно
и радостно дышится,

Nightingale

Hark,
the nightingale sings,
sings the songs
that are old as the ages...
His retirement
he surely presages!

For the nightingale's
aged and ill...
But then why,
when his song is vibrating,
everybody is flushed by a
                              thrill
souls exalt,
hearts begin palpitating.

Though a thousand years old,
still like new
seems his song,
as if only just written;
and it causes the grass
and the dew—
all of nature—
to stand
magic-smitten.

Though a thousand years old,
so alive
that our spirits
begin gaily singing,

в ней
почти человечьи слова,
отпечатавшись в воздухе,
слышатся!

Те слова
о бессмертье страстей,
о блаженстве,
предельном страданию;
будто нет на земле новостей
кроме тех,
что как мир стародавние.

Вот каков
этот старый певец,
заклинающий
звездною клятвою...
Песнь утихнет,
и страсти конец
и сердца
разбиваются надвое!

and its human-like accents
revive
words that once
in our bosoms were ringing.

Words of passions eternal
and thought,
words of bliss
and of great tribulations,
as if news on the earth there is naught,
save for that
which is old as creation.

Such is the power
of this bird of renown
that the stars in the sky
stop in wonder...
Song dies out
and all passions cool down,
and our hearts
are all broken asunder!

Translated by Eugene Felgenhauer

*Bella Akhmadulina (b. 1937) is a gifted young poetess.
She was educated at the Gorky Literary Institute
where she studied together with Yevgeni Yevtushenko
and Robert Rozhdestvensky. A collection of her poetry
came out in 1962. She also writes stories and film
scripts and acts in the cinema. In her graceful, plastic
poetry she responds with great subtlety of feeling to
people's happiness, suffering and hopes. Her verse is
like exquisite filigree work, its intricate patterns and
modulations reflecting the subtlest shades of feeling
and mood, sometimes as light as a fleeting sigh.*

BELLA AKHMADULINA

БЕЛЛА АХМАДУЛИНА

Декабрь

Мы соблюдаем правила зимы.
Играем мы, не уступая смеху,
и, придавая очертанья снегу,
приподнимаем белый снег с земли.

И, будто бы предчувствуя беду,
прохожие толпятся у забора,
снедает их тяжелая забота:
а что с тобой имеем мы в виду?

Мы бабу лепим, только и всего.
О, это торжество и удивленье,
когда и высота, и удлиненье
зависят от движенья твоего.

Ты говоришь: — Смотри, как я леплю. —
Действительно, как хорошо ты лепишь
и форму от бесформенности лечишь.
Я говорю: — Смотри, как я люблю.

Снег уточняет все свои черты
и слушается нашего приказа.
И вдруг я замечаю, как прекрасно
лицо, что к снегу обращаешь ты.

Проходим мы по белому двору,
мимо прохожих, с выраженьем дерзким.
С лицом таким же пристальным и детским
любимый мой, всегда играй в игру.

December

The rules of winter we obey.
We roll a snowball and run after,
Acclaim its growth with peals of laughter
And brush the surplus snow away.

As if misfortune were in view,
The people passing by assemble
Along the fence with lips atremble
To watch what you and I shall do.

We make a snowman—that is all!
O what a triumph when from under
Your hands appears the chosen wonder,
To your prescription, stout and tall!

You say: "Just look what I can do!"
I notice with what skill and passion
From formlessness new form you fashion
And say: "I love you, I love you!"

With what exactness snow can trace
The very features we intended!
Then suddenly I see resplendent,
The sidelong profile of your face.

Scorning the crowd we walk away
Across the yard with self-possession.
With such a child's intent expression
May you, beloved, always play!

Поддайся его долгому труду,
о моего любимого работа!
Даруй ему удачливость ребенка
рисующего домик и трубу.

To his long-lasting labour yield,
O handiwork of my beloved!
Grant the reward a child discovers
On painting flowers in a field!

Translated by Peter Tempest

Мотороллер

Завиден мне полет твоих колес,
о мотороллер розового цвета!
Слежу за ним, не унимая слез,
что льют без повода в начале лета.

И девочке, припавшей к седоку
с ликующей и гибельной улыбкой,
кажусь я приникающей к листку,
согбенной и медлительной улиткой.

Прощай! Твой путь лежит поверх меня
и меркнет там, в зеленых отдаленьях.
Две радуги, два неба, два огня,
бесстыдница, горят в твоих коленях.

И тело твое светится сквозь плащ,
как стебель тонкий сквозь стекло и воду
Вдруг из меня какой-то странный плач
выпархивает, пискнув, на свободу.

Так слабенький твой голосок поет,
и песенки мотив так прост и вечен.
Но, видишь ли, веселый твой полет
недвижностью моей уравновешен.

Затем твои качели высоки
и не опасно головокруженье,
что по другую сторону доски
я делаю обратное движенье.

Scooter

I watch the scooter's flight
And feel my envy growing!
My eyes are hot and bright
With summer's quick tears flowing

A girl with winning smile
Clings closely to the rider.
A humpy sluggish snail
Do I appear beside her.

Farewell! Ride at your ease
To where green summits glimmer.
Look, in your shameless knees
Two blazing rainbows shimmer.

Your body through the coat
Shines like a vase-clad flower.
A strange cry from my throat
Erupts with sudden power.

How soft the song you trill!
How simple the emotion!
My immobility
Matches your fleeting motion!

You ride your swing so high,
No dizziness discerning,
For on the other side
My swing is fast returning.

Пока ко мне нисходит тишина,
твой шум летит в лужайках отдаленных
Пока моя походка тяжела,
подъемлешь ты два крылышка зеленых.

Так проносись — я все еще стою.
Так лепечи — я все еще немею.
И легкость поднебесную твою
я искупаю тяжестью своею.

When all sound here is dead,
Far fields still hear you scutter.
How rude my heavy tread!
How light your green wings' flutter!

Speed on! Here I shall wait,
Talk fast! Dumb shall I be.
So shall my pose sedate
Redeem your levity.

Translated by Peter Tempest

*Anna Akhmatova (1889-1966). The classic dignity of
Akhmatova's beautiful poetry, in which even passion is
held in check by logic, is associated in the reader's
mind with the sombre wistfulness of Leningrad, the
splendours of its classic architecture and the cold gleam
of the Neva. For many years this poetess was known
mainly for her elegiac preoccupation with one theme—
the tragedy of a woman's infinite, unconsummated
love, the cry of a lonely soul for understanding and
sympathy. The Great Patriotic War broadened the range
of her themes. Akhmatova's wartime and post-war
poetry speaks of history, patriotism and human solidar-
ity. Her writing is not flamboyant, her words and
images are simple, and she leaves a great deal unsaid
but merely hinted at. Spiritual phenomena, such as
memory, dreams or fantasies, are so perfectly sculptured
that they become tangible things. Shortly before she
died Anna Akhmatova received the Taormina Prize,
and a few weeks after that she was singled out to receive
an honorary degree of Oxford University.*

ANNA AKHMATOVA

АННА АХМАТОВА

Наше священное ремесло
Существует тысячи лет...
С ним и без света миру светло.
Но еще ни один не сказал поэт,
Что мудрости нет, и старости нет
А может, и смерти нет.

Our sacred craft has existed
For thousands of years....
With it, luminous even in darkness is earth
But no poet has ever insisted,
Through laughter or tears,
That there is no wisdom, no age, no death.

Translated by Irina Zheleznova

Родная земля

*И в мире нет людей бесслезней
Надменнее и проще нас.*

1922

В заветных ладанках не носим на груди,
О ней стихи навзрыд не сочиняем,
Наш горький сон она не бередит,
Не кажется обетованным раем.
Не делаем ее в душе своей
Предметом купли и продажи,
Хворая, бедствуя, немотствуя на ней,
О ней не вспоминаем даже.
    Да, для нас это грязь на калошах,
    Да, для нас это хруст на зубах.
    И мы мелем, и месим, и крошим
    Тот ни в чем не замешанный прах.
Но ложимся в нее и становимся ею,
Оттого и зовем так свободно — своею.

This Russian Soil

In all the world no people are so tearless,
So proud, so simple as are we.

1922

In lockets for a charm we do not wear it,
In verse about its sorrows do not weep,
With Eden's blissful vales do not compare it,
Untroubled does it leave our bitter sleep.
To traffic in it is a thought that never,
Not even in our hearts, remote, takes root.
Before our eyes its image does not hover,
Though we be beggared, sick, despairing, mute.
    It's the mud on our shoes, it is rubble,
    It's the sand on our teeth, it is slush,
    It's the pure, taintless dust that we crumble,
    That we pound, that we mix, that we crush.
But we call it our own for 'twill open one day
To receive and embrace us and turn us to clay.

Translated by Irina Zheleznova

Тринадцать строчек

Из цикла „ПОЛНОЧНЫЕ СТИХИ"

И наконец ты слово произнес
Не так, как те... что на одно колено —
А так, как тот, кто вырвался из плена
И видит сень священную берез
Сквозь радугу невольных слез.
И вкруг тебя запела тишина,
И чистым солнцем сумрак озарился,
И мир на миг один преобразился,
И странно изменился вкус вина.
И даже я, кому убийцей быть
Божественного слова предстояло,
Почти благоговейно замолчала,
Чтоб жизнь благословенную продлить.

Thirteen Lines

From the cycle POEMS OF MIDNIGHT

You spoke at last...
                        No wooer on bended knees
Those words, those fateful words would thus
                                          have spoken...
You said them like a captive who has broken
His chains, and fled, and through the blur of tears
A virgin grove of nodding birches sees.
The silence sang and hummed; the sun's pure blaze
Cut through the shadows, and the darkness banished;
The wine's flat taste had changed; the present vanished;
A world transformed by magic met your gaze.
And I who was to be a murderess,
I, cruelly doomed that fragile dream to shatter,
Sought to prolong it and refused to utter
The brutal words that would destroy such bliss.

Translated by Irina Zheleznova

Не стращай меня грозной судьбой
И великою северной скукой.
Нынче праздник наш первый с тобой
И зовут этот праздник — разлукой.
Ничего, что не встретим зарю,
Что луна не блуждала над нами,
Я сегодня тебя одарю
Небывалыми в мире дарами:
Отраженьем моим на воде
В час, как речке вечерней не спится,
Взглядом тем, что падучей звезде
Не помог в небеса возвратиться,
Эхом голоса, что изнемог,
А тогда был и свежий и летний, —
Чтоб ты слышать без трепета мог
Воронья подмосковного сплетни,
Чтобы сырость октябрьского дня
Стала слаще, чем майская нега...
Вспоминай же, мой ангел, меня,
Вспоминай хоть до первого снега.

Do not speak of the north and its sadness
And a dread and malevolent fate.
Surely this is a festive occasion:
You and I, we are parting today.
Never mind that the moon will not haunt us,
And the dawn you and I will not meet.
I will shower you with gifts, my beloved,
Of a kind that have never been seen.
Take my wavering, dancing reflection
In the shimmery glass of a stream;
Take my gaze that the great, swooning stars
As they fall from the heavens arrests;
Take my voice, take its spent, broken echo,
Once so summery, youthful and fresh....
Take my gifts: they will help you to listen
Without pain to the gossiping birds
In the wet of a Moscow October,
And will turn autumn's gloom to the languor
And the sweetness of May.... O, my angel,
Think of me, think of me till the first
Flakes of snow start to waltz in the air....

Translated by Irina Zheleznova

Три стихотворения

1

Пора забыть верблюжий этот гам
И белый дом на улице Жуковской.
Пора, пора к березам и грибам,
К широкой осени московской.
Там всё теперь сияет, всё в росе,
И небо забирается высоко,
И помнит Рогачевское шоссе
Разбойный посвист молодого Блока...

2

И в памяти черной, пошарив, найдешь
До самого локтя перчатки.
И ночь Петербурга. И в сумраке лож
Тот запах и душный и сладкий.
И ветер с залива. А там, между строк,
Минуя и ахи и охи,
Тебе улыбнется презрительно Блок —
Трагический тенор эпохи.

3

Он прав — опять фонарь, аптека,
Нева, безмолвие, гранит...

Three Poems

1

It's time!... Oh, to forget Zhukovsky Street,
The white-walled house, the city's roofs and arches
Its zoo-like din.... Away! Away to meet
The winking mushrooms and the nodding birches
Of Moscow's princely, sparkling, dewy fall,
The skies remote, the leaves and grasses rustling,
And Rogachevsky Highway throbbing still
With youthful Blok's untamed and reckless whistling

2

Sounding the dark depths of memory,
I find a St. Petersburg night, fluid and shimmery,
A theatre box's velvet-hung gloom
Haunted by smells that are chokingly warm,
Gusts of wind from the gulf, and, just as it was,
Scornful of all the "oh's" and the "ah's",
That arrogant smile, growing no dimmer,
That belonged to Blok,
      our epoch's tragic tenor.

3

How right he was—the lamp, the Neva,
The chemist's shop, and a mirage:

Как памятник началу века,
Там этот человек стоит —
Когда он Пушкинскому Дому
Прощаясь, помахал рукой
И принял смертную истому
Как незаслуженный покой.

A man, a monument erected
To mark the advent of our age....
He glimpsed it all again the evening
To Pushkin's house he waved goodbye,
And like a rest he did not merit
Embraced death's wearing agony.

Translated by Irina Zheleznova

Четвертая

Есть три эпохи у воспоминаний.
И первая — как бы вчерашний день.
Душа под сводом их благословенным,
И тело в их блаженствует тени.
Еще не замер смех, струятся слезы,
Пятно чернил не стерто со стола
И, как печать на сердце, поцелуй —
Единственный, прощальный, незабвенный.
Но это продолжается недолго...
Уже не свод над головой, а где-то
В глухом предместье дом уединенный,
Где холодно зимой, а летом жарко,
Где есть паук, и пыль на всем лежит,
Где истлевают пламенные письма,
Исподтишка меняются портреты,
Куда, как на могилу, ходят люди,
А возвратившись, моют руки мылом
И стряхивают беглую слезинку
С усталых век — и тяжело вздыхают...
Но тикают часы, весна сменяет
Одна другую, розовеет небо,
Меняются названья городов,
И нет уже свидетелей событий,
И не с кем плакать, не с кем вспоминать
И медленно от нас уходят тени,
Которых мы уже не призываем,
Возврат которых был бы страшен нам.
И, раз проснувшись, видим, что забыли
Мы даже путь в тот дом уединенный

The Fourth

From the cycle NORTHERN ELEGIES

One's memories live long and have three epochs.
The first is close, like yesterday.... Within
Its hallowed bower the soul enjoys repose,
And in its shade the body refuge finds....
The tears stream still, the peals of laughter

linger,

The spot of ink still stains the desk, and, sealed
Upon the heart, the farewell kiss remains,
Indelible.... But this is not for long....
The bower recedes, and in its place there stands
A lonely house, unswept and hung with cobwebs,
Where it is cold in winter, and in summer
Insufferably hot, where lovers' letters
Turn brown with dust, and treasured pictures fade
Where people come as to a grave to lay
A wreath of flowers, and, afterwards, at home,
Scrub at their hands with soap, and brush away
A fleeting tear, and sigh, and sigh again.
But clocks tick on, and seasons come and go,
The names of cities change, events retain
No witnesses, and memories and tears
May not be shared.... Unwanted and unsought,
The shades of loved ones shrink and slip away,
And we recoil in horror from the thought
That they might reappear.... And then the day
Dawns when, awakening with a start, and gripped
With sickening remorse, we realise
That we no longer know where lies the path
To that lone house, and run as in a dream,

И, задыхаясь от стыда и гнева,
Бежим туда, но (как во сне бывает)
Там всё другое: люди, вещи, стены,
И нас никто не знает — мы чужие!
Мы не туда попали... Боже мой!
И вот тогда горчайшее приходит:
Мы сознаем, что не могли б вместить
То прошлое в границы нашей жизни,
И нам оно почти что так же чуждо,
Как нашему соседу по квартире;
Что тех, кто умер, мы бы не узнали,
А те, с кем нам разлуку бог послал,
Прекрасно обошлись без нас — и даже
Все к лучшему...

Despairing mute, to where it stood, and lo!—
Discover that the walls, the things, the people
Are different and strange, and that we too
Are strangers there.... The bitter revelation
Then comes that we must shed the hope of

fitting

The past into the pattern of our lives
For it is alien to ourselves, the way
It needs must be to someone in the street....
And then we know and are repelled at knowing
That if the dead, by any chance, returned
We should not know them, that the cherished few
With whom God chose to part us, miss us not,
That it is better so, that it is all,
Perversely, for the best....

Translated by Irina Zheleznova

Olga Bergholtz (b. 1910) is the daughter of a Leningrad doctor. She grew up in that city and was educated at the State University there. Her life and her art are forever bound up with Leningrad, the cradle of the Revolution. In the grim days of the blockade she shared with her readers her last crust of bread and her last bit of warmth. Her "February Diary" and "Leningrad Poem" written in 1942 made her name a symbol of tragic art. "Loyalty" (1954)—a tragedy in verse—has been acclaimed as one of the greatest works of poetry produced in the last fifteen years. The theme of this tragedy is an appeal for trust in the people who in painful travail gave birth to the new, just world. Olga Bergholtz's poetry of these last few years is a passionate confession of our contemporary.

OLGA BERGHOLTZ

ОЛЬГА БЕРГГОЛЬЦ

Из писем с дороги

II

Я сердце свое никогда не щадила.
Ни в песне, ни в горе, ни в дружбе,
                              ни в страсти.
Прости меня, милый. Что было — то было.
Мне горько.
          И все-таки все это — счастье.

И то, что я страшно, горюче тоскую.
И то, что, страшась неизбежной напасти,
На призрак, на малую тень негодую.
Мне страшно.
          И все-таки все это — счастье.

О, пусть эти слезы и это удушье,
Пусть хлещут упреки, как ветки
                              в ненастье.

Страшней — всепрощенье. Страшней —
                              равнодушье
Любовь не прощает. и все это — счастье.

Я знаю теперь, что она убивает,
Не ждет состраданья, не делится властью.
Покуда прекрасна, покуда живая.
Покуда опа не утеха, а — счастье.

From a Wayfarer's Letters

II

I have treated my heart with a ruthless abandon
In poetry, in friendship, in grief and in passion.
Forgive me, my darling. Let bygones be bygones.
I suffer. Yet all this is joy in its fashion.

And even my black fits of burning depression,
The starting at shadows, the nervous reaction
To trifles which nourish my fearful obsession
With doom and disaster, are joy in their fashion.

I care not if I choke on these tears' salt insurgence
Reproaches may flay me, like wet branches lashing.
More fearful by far are indifference, indulgence.
Love never forgives, yet is joy—in its fashion.

For love brooks no rival, expects no compassion.
Love—now I know it—can kill and destroy,
Just so long as it's beautiful, live and impassioned,
Just so long as it's not a mere pastime, but joy.

Translated by Avril Pyman

V

А я вам говорю, что нет
напрасно прожитых мной лет,
ненужно пройденных путей,
впустую слышанных вестей.
Нет невоспринятых миров,
нет мнимо розданных даров,
любви напрасной тоже нет —
любви обманутой, больной,
ее нетленно чистый свет
всегда во мне,
           всегда со мной.
И никогда не поздно снова
начать всю жизнь,
           начать весь путь,
и так, чтоб в прошлом бы — ни слова
ни стона бы не зачеркнуть.

V

And this I solemnly declare:
That I have lived no worthless year,
Nor trodden any road for naught,
Nor closed my mind to any thought,
Nor closed my ears to any news,
Nor given gifts where none were due.
Neither do I my Love regret,
Deceived and wounded and unsure,
Whose light, imperishably pure,
Is with me yet,
                is in me yet.
And it will never be too late
To start afresh,
             begin again...
Yet from the past obliterate
No single word, no gasp of pain.

Translated by Avril Pyman

Бабье лето

Есть время природы особого света,
неяркого солнца, нежнейшего зноя.
Оно называется

бабье лето
и в прелести спорит с самою весною.

Уже на лицо осторожно садится
летучая, легкая паутина...
Как звонко поют запоздалые птицы!
Как пышно и грозно пылают куртины!

Давно отгремели могучие ливни,
все отдано тихой и темною нивой...
Все чаще от взгляда бываю счастливой,
все реже и горше бываю ревнивой.

О мудрость щедрейшего бабьего лета,
с отрадой тебя принимаю... И все же,
любовь моя, где ты, аукнемся, где ты?
А рощи безмолвны, а звезды все строже...

Вот видишь — проходит пора звездопада,
и, кажется, время навек разлучаться...
А я лишь теперь понимаю, как надо
любить, и жалеть, и прощать,

и прощаться

Indian Summer*

There's a season alight with its own, strange shimmer
Of misted sun, most tenderly warm.
People call it
        Indian summer
And it rivals the spring itself in charm.

Already the flying gossamer's clinging
Lightly, warily round the face...
How full is the tone of the late birds' singing!
How fierce and festive the flower-beds blaze!

The great rains have long since passed in thunder,
The dark, silent field has yielded its all...
More often a glance strikes a spark of wonder
More seldom, but blacker the jealous fits fall.

O generous wisdom of Indian summer,
I welcome you gratefully, but: Do you hear,
My lost love, where are you? Where are you? Come, answer!
But the woods have grown silent, the stars more
                austere...

You see now—the season of stardust is over.
I suppose it is time that we parted—and yet
It is only just now I've begun to discover
How to love and to cherish, forgive—
               and forget.

Translated by Avril Pyman

* In Russian Indian summer is called "Woman's summer"

Petrus Brovka (b. 1905). The work of this well-known Byelorussian poet provides a fine example of the folk-song trend in Soviet poetry. His lyricism is rooted in his native Byelorussia and conveys the inimitable colours of its woods and fields, the clear sparkle of its rivers and the bustle of its cities Petrus Brovka loves folk themes, simple language and song-like rhythms. It is not surprising that music has been written to many of his verses. His volume of poetry "And Time Goes On" won him the Lenin Prize in 1962. Petrus Brovka is also well known as a translator of Russian and Ukrainian poetry into Byelorussian.

PETRUS BROVKA

ПЕТРУСЬ БРОВКА

Начало

Над нами тосты не гремели,
Когда мы только в жизнь вошли.
Лишь матери у колыбелей
Вздыхали, пели, как могли.

И на работу поневоле
С собой таскали нас они.
Под шелест жита, в знойном поле
Укладывали нас в тени.

Весь день в работе. Но и ночью
Не наступал покоя час.
— Усни, кровинка. Спи, сыночек!
Они укачивали нас.

Порой не до кормежки сына, —
Полно у матери хлопот, —
И суслом хлебно-сахаринным
Младенцу затыкали рот.

Нас без присмотра оставляли
В горячке деревенских дел
И лишь потуже пеленали,
Чтоб малый на пол не слетел.

Пеленки нас не удержали,
Мы на ноги сумели встать,
И босиком мы начинали
По колкому жнивью ступать.

Life's Beginning

There were no toasts, no loaded tables,
No songs were sung when we were born,
And just our mothers at our cradles
Crooned over us a tune forlorn.

They carried us to work each day,
With none an eye on us to keep,
And while they stacked and forked the hay
They left us in the shade to sleep.

They toiled till dark and knew no rest
When night-time came and day was done,
For then they rocked us at their breast
And hushed us: "Sleep, my baby son."

Some days they could not nurse or mind us
And so we wouldn't fret or weep
They stopped our mouths with pacifiers—
Rag dummies soaked in syrup sweet.

When harvest-time was at its height
They could not take us to the farm,
They left us, bundled very tight,
And prayed we wouldn't come to harm.

We wriggled free and crawled outside
Into the sunlight and the heat,
And on the prickly stubble tried
To learn to walk on shoeless feet.

Все было в мире незнакомо,
Все поражало нас кругом —
И встречи первые у дома
С котом, собакой, петухом,

И гром, и летние зарницы,
И сельской ночи тишина,
И бора шум, и звон криницы,
И августовская луна.

Росли мы... Дни текли за днями
Окрепли руки, плечи, грудь.
Омыты щедрыми дождями,
Утершись чистыми ветрами,
Мы выходили в дальний путь.

The world seemed strange and very new,
All things look different when you walk,
Familiar things you thought you knew:
The cat, the chickens, and the dog...

And stranger still—the rustling trees,
The moon, the thunder and the rain,
The silence and the rising breeze,
The creaking of the bucket chain...

Day followed day... The years rolled on.
Our shoulders broadened, arms grew strong.
With faces washed by many rains,
Dried in the morning wind and sun,
We started out upon our own.

Translated by Olga Shartse

Дубовый лист

Я не страшусь
Ненастья злого,
Перед метелью устою —
За жизнь держусь, как лист дубовый
За ветку держится свою.

В осенней мгле,
В промозглой хмури
Он полыхает, словно медь,
Чтобы в ответ на посвист бури
Раскачиваться
И звенеть.

Когда зимою
Вьюга стонет
И злобно щерится мороз,
Он прикрывает, как ладонью,
Ту ветку,
На которой рос.

Но, вешней зорькой
Околдован,
Он, встретив солнечный восход,
Уступит место листьям новым
И тихо наземь
Упадет.

The Oakleaf

The darkest clouds won't terrify me,
I can withstand the fiercest winds,
I cling to life, all storms defying,
As to its branch an oakleaf clings.

Through autumn rain and gloom despairing
It blazes with a copper glint,
And when a vicious wind comes tearing
The oakleaf merely sways and rings.

In winter, when the cold turns mean
And every night a blizzard blows,
The oakleaf valiantly screens
The mother branch on which it grows.

But when the spring its magic weaves
The oakleaf welcomes it, enthralled,
And ceding place to young green leaves
Upon the ground it softly falls.

Translated by Olga Shartse

Ojars Vācietis (b. 1933) is a Latvian poet. His poetry first appeared in print in 1950. Since then he has published the following collections: "The wind of Distant Roads" (1956), "Under Fire" (1958) and "Meridian Through the Heart" (1959). His openly committed, free verse reflects the changes in the life of his country. Vācietis did for modern Latvian poetry what Yevtushenko did for Russian: he addressed the broad public, speaking to them as a publicist on topical, vitally important problems. His later work shows a more lyrical approach to life and the world around him.

OJARS VACIETIS

ОЯР ВАЦИЕТИС

Перед операцией

Товарищ врач!
Незаконно.
Нагло.
Но последний день, очевидно,
Как гоминдановец в Организации
                              Объединенных Наций,
В груди моей сидит осколок.
          Я уже в годах.
          И потому не берусь утверждать,
          Что снаряд сделал фашист —
          Может быть.

          А быть может, немецкий рабочий
          Или пленный, мой однополчанин,
          Косясь на дуло парабеллума.
Я ношу его с той дымящейся груды
                              развалин,
Что раньше называлось —
Варшава.

И с этого дня
На два-три грамма
Врут все весы,
На которых я взвешиваюсь.

          Особых жалоб нет.
          Осколок вел себя довольно прилично
          Только два раза напомнил о себе
          Так, что дух захватило.

Before the Operation

Comrade Doctor!
Illicitly,
Shamelessly,
But evidently for the last day,
A shell splinter's lurking in my heart.
    I'm no longer young
    And, therefore, do not undertake to claim
    That shell was made by a fascist—
    May be, it was.
    Or, maybe, a German worker
    Or a P.O.W., my brother soldier
    Made it, looking askance at a pistol
                          barrel.
I've been carrying it from that smoking heap
of ruins
That once was called
Warsaw.

And since that day,
All the scales
On which I weighed myself
Have always lied, showing several grammes
Too much.

I have no special complaints.
The splinter has behaved quite decently.
Only twice did it remind me of itself,
So that I had to gasp for breath.

Первый —
Когда, вернувшись с победой домой,
Я забыл, целуясь,
Сколько мне лет.

Второй —
Когда падало с машины бревно
И я думал,
Что удержу его.

Товарищ врач!
После операции я прошу
Вернуть мне этот осколок.
Он жил по соседству с сердцем,
Стенка была тоньше папиросной бумаги
И он все подслушал.

А самое главное —
Нельзя отпускать на свободу осколки,
Которые побывали в груди у человека
И знают туда дорогу.

Once—
When I came home a victor,
And,
giving and receiving kisses,
Forgot my age.
And next—
When a log slipped from a truck
And I tried to hold it.
    Comrade doctor!
    After the operation,
    Please give that splinter back to me.
    It has lived so long right next to my heart,
    Separated from it by a space
    Thinner than cigarette paper,
    And has overheard everything.
But the main thing, however,
Is, that splinters that have penetrated
Human breasts and know the way in,
Should never be let free.

Translated by Louis Zellikoff

Напутствие

Сын, это я —
Земля, твоя планета.
Не ведаю,
Достигнут ли тебя всегда и всюду
Моих радиостанций маяки,
Не ведаю,
Металл моих ракет
Всегда и всюду выстоять ли сможет

Ты выстоишь.
Ведь ты мой сын,
В тебя не верить — значит
Не уважать
Своих вершин и облаков седины.

Я — мать,
И от тебя не оторвать мне рук.
Моя любовь
Тебя в ракете не оставит,
И пальцы мои силой притяженья
Тебя притянут,
Ибо ты мне дорог.

A Valediction

Son, this is I—
Your native planet.
I do not know
If the waves of my radio stations
Will always be received everywhere.
I do not know
If the steel of my rockets
Will always and everywhere endure.

You will endure.
You are my son,
And not to believe in you
Is not to believe
In my own hoary peaks and clouds.

When trains pull out, I feel no pain;
When ships put out to sea, my heart does not ache
But, when the space rocket starts,
My love for you
Will throb...

I am your mother
And cannot tear my hands
Away from you.
My love
Will press you down to your seat in the rocket,
My hands will pull you back
With all the strength
Of my heart's love.

Но ты не слушай моего призыва —
«Останься!»
Слушай только —
«Возвратись скорее!»
Со звездной пылью на подошвах —
Вернись!

Со звездным отражением в глазах -
Вернись!
Со звездною тревогой в сердце —
Вернись!

Вдоль побережий рек моих пройдут
Упругие тропинки.
Дожди прольются,
И, словно волосы твоей любимой,
Благоухая,
Пронизанная грозовым озоном,
Распустится моя сирень.

Сын, это я,
Земля, твоя планета,
Возьми с собою в звездную дорогу
Ковригу моего ржаного хлеба
И горсть земли.

Do not heed my
"Don't go..."
But hearken to my
"Return!"

With starlight in your eyes,
Return.
With starry passion in your blood,
Return.
With stardust clinging to your feet,
Return.

The banks of my rivers,
Woven with firm-trodden paths
And my spring showers
will greet you;
And like your darling's tresses after rain,
So will my lilac
Overflow with its own fragrance
And the odour of the storm.

Son, this is I—
Your native planet.
Before you set off on your starbound flight,
Take a piece of my bread
And a handful of me
With you.

Translated by Louis Zellikoff

Aaron Vergelis (b. 1918), a Jewish poet, who grew up in the Ukraine, entered the literary scene in 1935. His most important books are "At the Spring" (1940), "Thirst" (1956), "Second Meeting" (1961) and "Poem of Space" (1962). Vergelis, a publicist and a critic, is the chief editor of the magazine "Soviet Motherland" published in Yiddish. In his poetry Vergelis traces the development of man's sense of civil responsibility.

AARON VERGELIS

АРОН ВЕРГЕЛИС

День открытых сердец

„...Объявляется день
открытых дверей".

Сердец открытых объявляю день я!
Кто хочет, пусть войдет хоть на мгновенье
но может оставаться и навек он
в моей душе.
С хорошим человеком
сживется сердце и во всем поладит,
а скверного само оно отвадит.

Не суйтесь в сердце, лица в масках. Сердце
захлопнется за вами, точно дверца
железной клетки. В сердце мне не лезьте
ни для запугиванья,
ни для лести.
Поймите: в сердце, для друзей просторном,
нет места для субъектов с сердцем черным.

Предупредил так одного-другого —
и убрались бродяги из-под крова,
но сердце не осталось сиротою —
стал круг теснее, но просторней вдвое.
Сердец открытых объявляю день я, —
кто хочет,
пусть заходит без стесненья!

Хожу полями, чащами лесными.
Иду,
не прячась под чужое имя;
к друзьям своим иду и не таюсь я,
и говорить открыто не боюсь я.

A Day of Open Hearts

A day of open hearts hereby declare I!
Welcome are all! However momentary
The visit, there'll be some who shall forever
Stay close to me.
For it is hard to sever
The bonds that to a good man bind one tightly,
While parting from a wicked man comes lightly.

Do not intrude with faces that are masked.
For straight behind you shall my heart lock fast
Its iron door. Do not ingratiate
Hoping to flatter
Or intimidate.
Know well: a heart has room for all true friends
But none for those who follow evil ends.

I've warned some few this way—and out of shelter
The scoundrels have gone running helter-skelter.
Their loss is little grief, no great disorder—
The circle closes but the ring is broader.
A day of open hearts hereby declare I!
Welcome are all!
Let none be shy, none tarry!

I walk through meadows and through forest clearing.
Under no borrowed name
I go unfearing,
I visit friends of mine, I am quite open,
In all I wish to say, I am outspoken.

107

С людьми встречаюсь на путях-дорогах,
и появляюсь на чужих порогах,
и разговариваю на распутье:
— Открыто сердце,
в нем как дома будьте!
Дружить давайте, — говорю я людям, —
вот так, все вместе, счастье раздобудем.
Сердец открытых объявляю день я, —
кто хочет, пусть заходит без стесненья!

Иду на площади, иду я в скверы,
стремлюсь в моря, в заоблачные сферы.
И всюду люди мне спешат навстречу.
«Открыто сердце?» — вот о чем их речи.
«Открыто!»
И вступают шагом смелым
и чернокожие, и люди с белым телом,
с глазами серыми и с голубыми.
Заходят старцы вместе с молодыми;
кто здоровенны, кто не так плечисты,
но главное — чтоб руки были чисты,
и только б сердца не черствила злоба,
и чтоб с гнилой душой ни одного бы!

Свободный, сильный,
с непомеркшим взором,
я по далеким шествую просторам:
мне с малышами нянчиться отрада,
в лугах пасу я с пастухами стадо.
Любые небеса гостеприимны —
повсюду песни и повсюду гимны.

Ждут люди, чтобы их благословили.
И я хочу, чтоб в людях люди жили.
И лишь злодей
надеяться на милость
не смей!
Для злобы сердце не открылось!
Уж если день сердец открытых — это
день, чтобы в сердца вошли потоки света
И я хочу, чтоб свет вошел туда
навечно, бесконечно, навсегда!

All sorts of people on the road I'm meeting,
To other people's homes I take my greeting
And always say when I resume my roaming:
"My open heart
"Is yours to feel at home in!"

"People, let's all be friends!" is what I tell them
"We'll win our happiness like this—together!"
A day of open hearts hereby declare I!
Welcome are all!
Let none be shy, none tarry!

Translated by Peter Tempest

Yevgeni Vinokurov (b. 1925) is one of the most gifted Russian poets to have appeared in the last twenty years or so. He was still a boy at school when the Second World War broke out. He joined up as a volunteer, and it was at the front that he began to write poetry. After the war he enrolled at the Literary Institute and graduated in 1951. His first book of verse was called "A Man's Duty". His "hero's" spiritual maturity grows with each new book, reflecting a compatible process taking place in the life of the poet's own generation. Vinokurov's poetry is a blend of philosophic symbolism, humour, and a truthful rendering of details taken from life around him. His latest books "World", "Music" and "Characters" (1961-1966) are a poetical encyclopedia of modern man's emotions, feelings and thoughts, clothed in plastic, dimensional images, and subjected to a profound psychological analysis.

YEVGENI VINOKUROV

ЕВГЕНИЙ ВИНОКУРОВ

Кто только мне советов не давал!
Мне много в жизни выдалось учебы.
А я все только головой кивал:
— Да, да, конечно! Ясно! Ну, еще бы

Поднявши   перст,
                              кто только не держал
Меня за лацкан!
                      — Да, ага, понятно!
Спасибо! Ладно!
                      — Я не возражал:
Ну что мне стоит.
                              А ведь им приятно...
— Да, да, согласен! Ой ли! Ей-же-ей!
Ну да, пожалуй! Вы правы, не скрою..

Чем больше слушал я учителей,
Тем больше я хотел быть сам собою.

I've had advice from everyone I know,
It was bestowed most subtly and astutely.
And all I did was nod my head: "That's so.
You're right.... You're right, old fellow,
                                    absolutely!"

One finger stiffly raised,
                            they'd clutch me tight
By the lapel.
            "I'm grateful beyond measure."
I never argued:
                "Yes... Yes, thank you....
                                    Quite."
It cost me nothing, and it gave them pleasure.
"I do agree.... I do... That's really clever!...
Without a doubt!... Of course.... I'll think it over...."

The harder did they try to shape my mind,
The more to be myself was I inclined.

                        Translated by Irina Zheleznova

Поэт бывал и нищим и царем.
Морским бродягой погибал на море.
Ушастым клерком он скрипел пером,
Уныло горбясь за полночь в конторе.
Повешен был за кражу, как Вийон.
Придворный, в треуголке, при параде,
Он фрейлин в ручку чмокал, умилен,
И с песней умирал на баррикаде.
Слепец брел рынком. Гусли. Борода.
По звонким тропам мчался по Кавказу
Но кем бы ни бывал он, никогда
Ни в чем не изменил себе ни разу.

Some poets begged for alms, some wielded sceptres;
Some pirated the seas; some, like Villon,
Were hanged for theft; some over musty ledgers
In gloomy offices sat poring; some till dawn
At balls of state in powdered wigs paraded
And danced the minuet with polished ease;
Some died on barricades; with psalteries
Some walked the roads; to some the hoary ranges
Of Caucasus spelt respite from the past....
And yet, though different their fates, through storms
and dangers
True to themselves they stayed until the last.

Translated by Irina Zheleznova

* * *

Крестились готы. В водоем до плеч
Они входили с видом обреченным.
Но над собой они держали меч,
Чтобы кулак остался некрещеным.
Быть должен и у кротости предел,
Что б заповедь смиренья ни гласила...
И я кулак бы сохранить хотел.
Я буду добр. Но в нем пусть будет сила

The Goths of old at baptism meekly wore
A look of doom.... But when the holy waters
Washed over them, aloft they held their swords,
Their fists unbaptised left for ever after.

Whatever the commandment's stern behest,
Humility, like patience, has its limit.
Though kind at heart, yet clenched I'll keep my fist—
And may there be the strength of metal in it.

Translated by Irina Zheleznova

Музыка

Стихия музыки — могучая стихия,
Она чем непонятней, тем сильней.
Глаза мои, бездонные, сухие,
Слезами наполняются при ней.

Она и невидна, и невесома,
И мы ее в крови своей несем...
Мелодии всемирная истома,
Как соль в воде, растворена во всем.

Покинув помещенья нежилые,
Вселившись в дом высокий, как вокзал
Все духи музыки — и добрые и злые —
Безумствуют, переполняя зал.

Сурова нитка музыкальной пьесы —
Верблюд, идущий сквозь ушко иглы.
Все бесы музыки, все игровые бесы,
Играючи, хотят моей игры.

Есть в музыке бездумное начало,
Призыв к свободе от земных оков.
Она не зря лукаво обольщала
Людей на протяжении веков.

Вакханки в исступлении зверели,
В поля бежали, руки заломив,
Лишь только на отверстия свирели
Орфей клал пальцы, заводя мотив.

Music

A mighty elemental force is music.
The more obscure is it, the greater is
The power it wields, the more is there
                      of magic
In every note.... Suffice it that it fills
My tearless eyes with tears....
                      A mellow languor,
It courses through the veins of humankind
And is, unseen, dissolved like salt in water
In everything.... Beneath a dome confined,
Its many spirits, kindly ones and evil,
Rebel and, frenzied, all our laws defy.
What is a piece of music but a camel
That passes through the needle's narrow eye! ...
Released, the demons prance and caper wildly
And to our senses lay delighted claim.
They call to us unthinkingly and blindly
To share, defenceless, in their frantic game.
They plead with us, these carefree, thoughtless
                      demons
Of worldly chains to break forever free.
For centuries has music's artful summons
Enticed the hearts of men unwittingly.
The bacchants, reeling, fled in mad abandon
Into the fields, and there did, drunken, stray
When, thoughtfully, a tune picked up at random
Would Orpheus on his pipe begin to play.

Но и сейчас, когда оркестр играет
Свою неимоверную игру,
Как нож с березы, он с людей сдирает
Рассудочности твердую кору.

And when, today, with sudden, tameless passion
A symphony rings out, it rends the dark,
And strips the sober mind of self-possession
The way a knife strips birch trees of their bark.

Translated by Irina Zheleznova

Andrei Voznesensky (b. 1933) was educated at an architectural institute. His first published work "The Masters" (1959) created a stir in the literary world and secured for him a place of importance among contemporary Russian poets. His books "Mosaics" and "Parabola" (both 1960) are dynamic, colourful and brilliant. In many of his poems the imagery is exaggeratedly complicated and startling. The nerve centre of his poetry is a feeling of alarm for the insecurity of the world in the atomic age. Yet at the same time Voznesensky is not a pessimist. In his later collections: "Forty Lyrical Digressions from the Poem "Triangular Pear" (1962), "Antiworlds" (1964) and "Oza" (1965) his furious denunciation of the world of lies, hypocrisy, violence and standardisation is based on humane principles of universal brotherhood. In 1963 Voznesensky wrote a poem about Lenin which he called "Longjumeau".

His poetry, with its syncopated rhythms and complex imagery, conveys more than the anxieties and painful stresses of our age: Voznesensky's sensitive awareness of beauty engenders hope and faith in life.

ANDREI VOZNESENSKY

АНДРЕЙ ВОЗНЕСЕНСКИЙ

Авиавступление

Из поэмы „ЛОНЖЮМО"

Вступаю в поэму, как в новую пору вступают
Работают поршни,

соседи в ремнях засыпают.
Ночной папироской

летят телецентры за Муром.
Есть много вопросов.

Давай с тобой, Время, покурим

Прикинем итоги.

Светло и прощально
горящие годы, как крылья, летят за плечами.
И мы понимаем, что канули наши кануны,
что мы да и спутницы наши —

не юны,
что нас провожают

и машут лукаво
кто маминым шарфом, а кто —

кулаками...

Земля,

ты нас взглядом апрельским проводишь,
лежишь на спине, по-ночному безмолвная.
По гаснущим рельсам

бежит

паровозик,
как будто

сдвигают

застежку

на «молнии».

Avia-Introduction

From the poem LONGJUMEAU

I start on my poem as though for an epoch unknown.
My neighbours doze off in their belts
                                    to the engine's
                                        smooth drone.
The Murom TV masts glow red
                        cigarettes in the night.
We've lots to discuss.
                    Have a smoke, Time, old man—
                                    here's a light

Let's cast up results.
                    Like meteors racing,
The years roll along, resplendent and blazing.
We know it's high time that a mass for our Springtime
                                        were sung
That we and our girlfriends
                        no longer are young,
That in seeing us off,
                    there are those who feign sadness—
Some wave Granny's shawl,
                        some their fists in their
                                        gladness.

O Earth,
        'tis of April your parting glance tells me
As, silent as night, on your back you repose.
A steam-engine
            runs on its rails
                        in the distance,
Just like the zipper
                that fastens
                        our clothes.

125

Россия, любимая,

с этим не шутят.
Все боли твои — меня болью пронзили.
Россия.

я — твой капиллярный

сосудик,
мне больно, когда —

тебе больно, Россия.

Как мелки отсюда успехи мои, неуспехи,
друзей и врагов кулуарных ватаги.
Прости меня,

Время,

что много сказать

не успею.
Ты, Время, не деньги,

но тоже тебя не хватает.

Но люди уходят, врезая в ночные отроги
дорог своих

огненные автографы!
Векам остаются — кому как удастся —
штаны — от одних,

от других — государства.

Е г о различаю.

Пытаюсь постигнуть,
чьим был этот голос с картавой пластинки.
Дай, Время, схватить этот профиль, паривший
в записках о школе его под Парижем.

Прости мне, Париж, невоспетых красавиц.
Россия,

прости незамятые тропки.
Простите за дерзость,

что я этой темы

касаюсь,
простите за трусость,

что я ее раньше не трогал

Вступаю в поэму. А если сплошаю,
прости меня, Время, как я тебе часто прощаю.

O Russia beloved,
                all this is no trifle—
Each pain felt by you pierces me with pain, too.
O Russia,
          I am
                your capillary vessel,
Whatever hurts me, Russia,
                            also pains you.

How petty from here my achievements and failures,
My friends and adversaries, dark lobbies packing:
Forgive me,
            O Time,
                    if at times
                                words fail me.
You Time, are not money—
                          yet you, too, are lacking

Men   pass
          and, in passing,
                           carve out their names
On the paths they have trodden
                                 in letters of flame:
To the Future some leave—as it pleases the Fates—
A pair of torn trousers,
                         others—whole states.

Now Him I distinguish,
                       in my mind, seek to see
The man who spoke, lisping from a record to me.
Time, help me to paint those features pervading
My notes on his school in a suburb of Paris.

Forgive me, O Paris, your beauties unsung.
O Russia,
          forgive me your pathways untrodden.

Forgive me my daring in touching this subject,
Forgive me for fearing
                       to touch it ere now.

I start on my poem. And if blunder I do,
Forgive me, O Time,
                    just as I pardon you.

Струится блокнот под карманным фонариком
Звенит самолет не крупнее комарика.

А рядом лежит

           в облаках алебастровых

планета —

        как Ленин,

               мудра и лобаста.

I pose o'er my notes in the light of
Like a tiny mosquito, our 'plane buz
And floating beside it,

in marble-whit(

Lies our planet—

like Lenin—

profound, lo(

Translated by Lou.

Параболическая баллада

Судьба, как ракета, летит по параболе
Обычно — во мраке и реже — по радуге.

Жил огненно-рыжий художник Гоген,
Богема, а в прошлом — торговый агент.
Чтоб в Лувр королевский попасть

из Монмартра

он
   дал

кругаля через Яву с Суматрой!

Унесся, забыв сумасшествие денег,
Кудахтанье жен, духоту академий.
Он преодолел

тяготенье земное.

Жрецы гоготали за кружкой пивною:
«Прямая — короче, парабола — круче,
Не лучше ль скопировать райские кущи?»

А он уносился ракетой ревущей
Сквозь ветер, срывающий фалды и уши.
И в Лувр он попал не сквозь главный порог —
Параболой

гневно

пробив потолок!

Идут к своим правдам, по-разному храбро,
Червяк — через щель, человек — по параболе.

Parabolical Ballad

Fortunes like rockets fly routes parabolical,
Rainbows less widespread than gloom diabolical.

For instance, the fiery-red painter Gaugin,
Bohemian, though sales-agent until then:
To get to the Louvre from nearby Montmartre
He looped through Tahiti, just missing Sumatra.

Sped skyward, forgetting of money-born madness,
Of cackling wives and of stifling academies.
And so
      he surmounted
               terrestrial gravity.

The priests of the fine arts were eager to have
                         at him
"A parabola's fine, but a straight line's far
                      shorter.
Better copy old Eden," they scoffed over porter.

But Gaugin zoomed away like today's rocketeers
In a wind that went tearing at coat-tails and ears
And entered the Louvre not through the front door,
But crashed his parabola through ceiling and floor!

Each reaches his truth with his own share
                        of nerve:
A worm through a chink
               and a man by a curve.

Жила-была девочка рядом в квартале.
Мы с нею учились, зачеты сдавали.
Куда ж я уехал!
                        И черт меня нес
Меж грузных тбилисских двусмысленных звезд!

Прости мне дурацкую эту параболу.
Простывшие плечики в черном парадном...
О, как ты звенела во мраке Вселенной
Упруго и прямо — как прутик антенны!
А я все лечу,
                        приземляясь по ним —
Земным и озябшим своим позывным.
Как трудно дается нам эта парабола!..

Сметая каноны, прогнозы, параграфы,
Несутся искусство,
                        любовь
                                и история —
По параболической траектории!

В сибирской весне утопают калоши
· · · · · · · · · ·
А может быть, все же прямая — короче?

There once lived a girl—just a few blocks away.
We took college together until one fine day.
Why on earth did I fly
                          like a blinking old ass
To mix with Tbilisi's ambiguous stars?

Don't blame me too hard for that barmy parabola,
Poor shoulders left out in the cold by a rambler!
How clear you rang out through the gloom of the
                                              universe
My slender antenna, in gales truly furious.
On and on I keep flying,
                          to land by your call,
My earthly antenna left out in the cold.
It's difficult business to fly a parabola.

Yet when art, love or history is the traveller,
Then, paragraphs, canons, prognoses defying,
Parabolical trajectories they go flying....

———————

Siberian spring drowns galoshes in water
. . . .
Perhaps, after all, though, a straight line
                                    is shorter?

                    Translated by Dorian Rottenberg

Осень в Сигулде

Свисаю с вагонной площадки,
прощайте,

прощай, мое лето,
пора мне,
на даче стучат топорами,
мой дом забивают дощатый,
прощайте,

леса мои сбросили кроны,
пусты они и грустны,
как ящик с аккордеона,
а музыку — унесли,

мы — люди,
мы тоже порожни,
уходим мы,
            так уж положено,
из стен,
        матерей
                и из женщин,
и этот порядок извечен,

прощай, моя мама,
у окон
ты станешь прозрачно, как кокон
наверно, умаялась за день,
присядем,

134

Autumn in Sigulda

Leaving, leaning out of a train
under the rain,

good-bye summer,
I've got to go....
Behind me they hammer
nails into shutters, blow after blow,
good-bye, I've got to go!

My woods are a vacant, joyless space—
no more leaves to doff—
like an accordion case
with the tunes carried off.

We people
are voided too,
we go when the time is due
from women, mothers, all in due course,
forced by eternal laws.

Good-bye, Mummy,
I won't be coming
so soon.
You'll stand there, transparent
                                    as a cocoon
worn out with the day.
Let's sit for a while till I start
                                    away.

о родина, попрощаемся,
буду звезда, ветла,
не плачу, не попрошайка,
спасибо, жизнь, что была,

на стрельбищах
в 10 баллов
я пробовал выбить 100,
спасибо, что ошибался,
но трижды спасибо, что

в прозрачные мои лопатки
входило прозренье, как
в резиновую
                перчатку
красный мужской кулак,

«Андрей Вознесенский» — будет,
побыть бы не словом, не бульдиком
еще на щеке твоей душной —
«Андрюшкой»,

спасибо, что в рощах осенних
ты встретилась, что-то спросила
и пса волокла за ошейник,
а он упирался,
спасибо,

я ожил, спасибо за осень,
что ты мне меня объяснила,
хозяйка будила нас в восемь,
а в праздники сипло басила
пластинка блатного пошиба,
спасибо,

но вот ты уходишь, уходишь,
как поезд отходит, уходишь...
из пор моих полых уходишь,
мы врозь друг из друга уходим,
чем нам этот дом неугоден?

ты рядом и где-то далеко,
почти у Владивостока,

Good-bye, my country, as well,
I'll be star or maybe fir,
I wont't cry for more—I've had my spell,
Thanks, life, that you were.

On targets for only ten points
I tried to score a hundred,
thanks for the way I blundered,
but thanks even more

that through my transparent shoulderblades
clairvoyance would shove
like a red male fist at first aid
through a rubber glove.

ANDREI VOZNESENSKY will come.
O to be not a word, not a bullying bum
but the least while more on your motherly cheek
your own Andryushka, soft and meek.

Thanks for the woods full of colour
where we met and roamed over knolls and banks
while you dragged your dog by the collar,
a stubborn old soul it was,
thanks,

I'm revived: so thanks for the autumn,
for explaining me to myself,
The landlady woke us at eight as she ought on
weekdays; on sundays it was like hell,
Her gramophone baring its fangs,
yet even for that
thanks.

But now you are leaving, moving away,
moving away like an out-going train,
leaving me vacant to fill with pain,
we're parting—going out of each other—
Parting again like me and mother.

You're beside me yet far away,
farther than words can say,

я знаю, что мы повторимся
в друзьях и подругах, в травинках
нас этот заменит и тот, —
«природа боится пустот»,

спасибо за сдутые кроны,
на смену придут миллионы,
за ваши законы — спасибо,

но женщина мчится по склонам,
как огненный лист за вагоном...

Спасите!

we'll all be repeated as years pass
in boyfriends and girlfriends and blades of grass
this, that or the other is bound to replace us,
nature won't tolerate blank spaces,

thanks for the trees gone bare,
millions will fill up the gap, so why care.
Thanks for the laws whose weight I've felt,

yet—
a woman speeds over hill and plain
like a flaming leaf in the wake of a train...
Help!

Translated by Dortan Rottenberg

Антимиры

Живет у нас сосед Букашкин,
Бухгалтер цвета промокашки.
Но, как воздушные шары,
Над ним горят

           Антимиры!

И в них магический, как демон,
Вселенной правит, возлежит
Антибукашкин, академик,
И щупает Лоллобриджид.

Но грезятся Антибукашкину
Виденья цвета промокашки.

Да здравствуют Антимиры!
Фантасты — посреди муры.
Без глупых не было бы умных,
Оазисов — без Каракумов.

Нет женщин —

              есть антимужчины
В лесах ревут антимашины.
Есть соль земли. Есть сор земли.
Но сохнет сокол без змеи.

Люблю я критиков моих.
На шее одного из них,
Благоуханна и гола,
Сияет антиголова!..

Antiworlds

Next door to us there lives a clerk
The colour of a watermark.
But above his knob, where he once had curls
Like air-balloons
           shine antiworlds!

And there, demoniac magician,
Assistant of the Lord Almighty,
An anti-clerk Academician
Lolls in the arms of Aphrodite.

But now and then the anti-clerk
Sees dreams the colour of a watermark.

Long live, long live ye antiworlds,
Fantastic among worlds absurd.
Without no fools there's be no sages.
No Saharas—no oases.

Women? No! Just anti-men.
Antimachines roar in the glen.
There's salt of earth, there's silt of earth.
Without the Earth the Sún's small worth.

My critics—I adore the lot.
One of the pack displays a pot
Bare as his knee and bright as lead—
A smacking, downright anti-head....

...Я сплю с окошками открытыми
А где-то свищет звездопад,
И небоскребы!
                 сталактитами
На брюхе глобуса висят.

И подо мной
              вниз головой,
Вонзившись вилкой в шар земной
Беспечный милый мотылек,
Живешь ты,
              мой антимирок!

Зачем среди ночной поры
Встречаются антимиры?

Зачем они вдвоем сидят
И в телевизоры глядят?

Им не понять и пары фраз.
Их первый раз — последний раз!

Сидят, забывши про бонтон,
Ведь будут мучиться потом!

И ушки красные горят,
Как будто бабочки сидят...

...Знакомый лектор мне вчера
Сказал: «Антимиры? Мура!»
Я сплю, ворочаюсь спросонок.
Наверно, прав научный хмырь...

Мой кот, как радиоприемник,
Зеленым глазом ловит мир.

By open windows I sleep nights
While somewhere else it's a day, they tell me,
With skyscrapers like stalactites
Suspended from the planet's belly.

And there, head down, at the Antipodes,
Pinned to the surface by the toes,
You live
          as carefree as a bird,
My own, my darling antiworld!

What makes two antiworlds at night
Gloat upon one another's sight?

Why do they sit like two twin pets,
Eyes glued to television sets?

They're deaf to all that's flying past.
Their first time is both first and last.

They sit, forgetting all bon-ton,
Though sure to suffer later on.

Just watch the way their red ears glow
Like butterflies, four in a row.

... My friend, a lecturer, passed word
That antiworlds were quite absurd.
So now by night I toss and turn,
Awaking from my sundry nightmares.

My cat's green eyes switch on and burn,
Catching the world, a feline wireless.

Translated by Dorian Rottenberg

Samuel Galkin (1897-1960) was a well-known Jewish poet, born in Byelorussia. He first appeared in print in 1922. His poetry, which takes the form of lyrical meditations, explores with insight and sympathy the fate of the ordinary, inconspicuous man. Both his lyric poems and his plays—"Bar-Cohba" (1939), "Salomith" (1940) and "Uprising in the Ghetto" (1947)—are very national in character. The tragedy of the Jewish people at different stages of history does not simply constitute the theme of his poems but sets the emotional tone to his entire work. Notes of gentleness, compassion, kindness and understanding for the grief of others are sounded in his later poetry, imbued with pure, noble and reserved emotion.

SAMUEL GALKIN

САМУИЛ ГАЛКИН

О корабле не судят по длине,
И клубы дыма — не его мерило.
Имеется в виду иная сила —
Насколько он тяжел морской волне.

Мерило, возведенное в закон, —
Объем воды, что вытесняет оп,
А я иначе мерю — сколь надежно
Он груз хранит от гибели возможной

A ship is judged not by its girth or grace
Nor by the volume of emitted smoke.
The yardstick used by ocean-going folk
Is just how heavy on the waves it weighs,

A measure canonised and worded in his law
By Archimedes many centuries before.
Yet I would ask — if anyone asked me—
How safe its cargo is from peril out at sea....

Translated by Dorian Rottenberg

В трудный день...

Когда подавлен я людской неправотой,
Где силу почерпнуть, чтобы равнялась той,
С какой убеждена — как будто впрямь чиста
В бесспорной правоте своей неправота?..

On Days of Stress

When down in spirits after men have done me wrong,
Where can I find the strength to be as strong
As are the wrong-doers, who all the facts despite
Are always certain they are doing right?

Translated by Dorian Rottenberg

Так вот она, старость... Закрытая дверь
Меж миром мечтанья и миром свершенья.
Все реже дано им сливаться теперь.
И даже в слиянии нет исцеленья.

Вот старость... Оцеплена, окружена
Флажками, как загнанный волк на поляне,
Кружится, но все не пробьется она
Из круга заклятого воспоминаний.

Вот старость... Гневливость без явных причин
Сто смыслов улыбки, теснящих друг друга.
Из всех этих смыслов понятней один:
Так чтит победителя сброшенный с круга.

So here's old age—a tight-shut door
Between the realms of act and dream.
More and more seldom than before
They merge in union supreme.

Old age ... surrounded, cornered in
By flags as if a hunted beast,
It seeks escape, but tears its skin
Against the nails of memories.

Old age ... rage without source or cause,
Smiles, meaning what? God only knows.
The clearest meaning to be found
Is—a victor's homage from the downed.

Translated by Dorian Rottenberg

И вот еще о чем моя тревога,
Мои сомнения, мой тайный страх:
Век нынешний — забот в нем было много
А радость люди выражали строго, —
Узнают ли мой век в моих стихах?

Быть может, скажет молодое племя:
Такую жизнь, мол, прожил человек,
А в чем, скажите, отразил он время,
Где каждый день был

                         точно стих в поэме
И вправе стать прославленным навек?..

Но иногда, все колебанья взвеся,
Я верю, что себя терзаю зря.
Как в сумерках замешана заря,
Мой век — в стихе моем, в его замесе.

И завтра иль поздней наступят сроки,
И в некий день безоблачно-высокий
Предстанет стих мой пред судом времен,
Печатью времени запечатлен.

Then it is this that fills me with concern,
A source of doubts, a cause for secret fears:
Far, far too many were the worries that could burn
A human heart in these distracting years
When even Joy's expression was too stern;

Will it be present in my poetry, our time,
Or will the coming generation say
The life he lived—where is it in his rhyme,
That age of turbulence whose every day
Was like a line of poetry sublime?

Yet somehow, when I weigh all con's and pro's
It seems that I torment myself in vain.
Just as the dawn of day in twilight shows,
Some inkling of these times my lines contain.

And so tomorrow or a later day will come,
A certain day of truly cloudless grandeur,
On which my poems will be judged by the full sum
Of time-born merits—to be duly praised or branded.

Translated by Dorian Rottenberg

Rasul Gamzatov (b. 1923) was born in the village which bears the name of his father Gamzat Tsadasa, People's poet of Daghestan. He was educated in Moscow, and began his career by translating the Russian classics into his native Avar language.

More than thirty books of poetry by Rasul Gamzatov have been translated into Russian and other languages. The popularity of his poetry is explained by its amazing and quite rare combination (Robert Burns can be given as an example) of natural talent, the tradition of naive ancient folk myths and songs and modern literary culture. Characteristic forms used by Rasul Gamzatov are the octave and the form of poetic, aphoristic "inscriptions", which Caucasian mountain dwellers used to engrave on the vaulted ceilings of their stone buildings, on tombstones, on sword handles and saddles.

In 1963 the poet was awarded the Lenin Prize.

RASUL GAMZATOV

РАСУЛ ГАМЗАТОВ

Утро и вечер, солнце и мрак —
Белый рыбак, черный рыбак.
В мире как в море; и кажется мне:
Мы, словно рыбы, плывем в глубине

В мире как в море, не спят рыбаки,
Сети готовят и ладят крючки.
В сети ли ночи, на удочку дня
Скоро ли время поймает меня?

Morning and evening, darkness and light—
Fishermen black and fishermen white.
The world's like an ocean; like fishes are we,
Like fishes that swim in the depths of the sea.

The world's like an ocean where fishermen wait,
Preparing their nets, their hooks and their bait.
How soon then, O Time, will you bring me to book
In the nets of the Night or on Day's baited hook?

Translated by Louis Zellikoff

Есть три заветных песни у людей,
И в них людское горе и веселье.
Одна из песен всех других светлеі
Ее слагает мать над колыбелью.

Вторая — тоже песня матерей.
Рукою гладя щеки ледяные,
Ее поют над гробом сыновей...
А третья песня — песни остальные

Three songs there be that thrill the human breast—
Three songs with human joy and sorrow laden.
And one of them is happier than the rest—
The song a mother sings beside a cradle.

The second by a mother, too, is sung—
Caressing icy cheeks with mourning fingers,
She sings it at the graveside of a son.
The third is sung by all the other singers.

Translated by Louis Zellikoff

У юноши из нашего аула
Была черноволосая жена,
В тот год, когда по двадцать
им минуло
Пришла и разлучила их война.

Жена двадцатилетнего героя
Сидит седая около крыльца.
Их сын, носящий имя дорогое,
Сегодня старше своего отца.

There was a lad who once lived in our village,
He had a youthful bride with raven hair,
That self-same year when she and he turned twenty
Came war, and tore him from his bride so fair.

The hero's bride is now a hero's widow.
Her hair is grey, her eyes have lost their fire;
Their son, who bears his father's name so precious,
Today is older than his fallen sire.

Translated by Louis Zellikoff

— Радость, помедли, куда ты летишь?
— В сердце, которое любит!
— Юность, куда ты вернуться спешишь?
— В сердце, которое любит!

— Сила и смелость, куда вы, куда?
— В сердце, которое любит!
— А вы-то куда, печаль да беда?
— В сердце, которое любит!

"Happiness—tarry; say whither you fly?"
"Into a loving heart."
"Youth, to return—whither haste you and why?"
"Into a loving heart."
"Courage and strength—tell me, whither and where?
"Into a loving heart."
"And whither haste YOU, O sorrow and care?"
"Into a loving heart."

Translated by Louis Zellikoff

Даже те, кому осталось, может,
Пять минут глядеть на белый свет
Суетятся, лезут вон из кожи,
Словно жить еще им сотни лет.

А вдали в молчаньи стовековом
Горы, глядя на шумливый люд,
Замерли, печальны и суровы,
Словно жить всего им пять минут.

Even some of those who have at best
Five short minutes left to live—no more,
Toil and moil without a minute's rest
As if they had some hundred years in store,

While snowy peaks, coeval with Creation,
In silence stern regarding petty Man,
Stand frozen still in mournful expectation
As if but five more minutes were their span.

Translated by Louis Zellikoff

Ты перед нами, время, не гордись,
Считая всех людей своею тенью.
Немало средь людей таких, чья жизнь
Сама источник твоего свеченья.

Будь благодарно озарявшим нас
Мыслителям, героям и поэтам.
Светилось ты и светишься сейчас
Не собственным, а их великим светом.

Stop boasting, time, that men are but your shadows
That all their grandeur just reflects your own.
'Tis men that lend their glory to their epoch,
Aye, men illumine time with their renown.

Be grateful to the poet, thinker, hero,
Who sheds on us the light of soul and mind.
The everlasting brilliance of an era
Emerges from the beacons of mankind.

Translated by Louis Zellikoff

Ты, время, вступаешь со мной в рукопашную
Пытаешь прозреньем, караешь презреньем,
Сегодня клеймишь за ошибки вчерашние
И крепости рушишь — мои заблужденья.

Кто знал, что окажутся истины зыбкими?
Чего же смеешься ты, мстя и карая,
Ведь я ошибался твоими ошибками,
Восторженно слово твое повторяя!

O Time, you pursue me with legions of terrors
With painful disclosure, disfavour, dismay;
Today you denounce me for Yesterday's errors
And smash my delusions like castles of clay.

Who knew that old truths were so easily shaken?
Then why do you laugh at me, why such unkindness?
I erred in the things in which you were mistaken,
Repeating your words in my rapturous blindness!

Translated by Louis Zellikoff

Ivan Drach (b. 1936) numbers among the Ukraine's gifted modern poets. He was educated at Kiev University and upon graduation worked first as a teacher and then as a newspaper correspondent. His first published collection "Sunflower" (1960) invited attention to his striking personality and the intelligence, originality, and metaphoric boldness of his poetry. His next book "The Solar Prominences of the Heart" (1965) evoked much discussion in the press. Drach is seeking his own ways of developing modern poetic diction and in doing so draws on the wealth of the Ukrainian language. He is an innovator not only as regards form (involved issociational lines, musically picturesque expressiveness, original rhythms) but also as regards content. Drach's poetry, in which he strives to bring out the general in the personal, and the universal in the national, is notable for the wide range of interests it embraces, for its intellectual depth.

IVAN DRACH

ИВАН ДРАЧ

Баллада о ведре

Я — форма из цинка. Мое содержанье —
Тяжелые шарики пыльной черешни,
Багряные зори на них задержались,
Теперь они дремлют во мне, захмелевши

Я — форма. Мое содержание — груши,
Соперницы солнца, светильники сада,
Республики Соков заблудшие души,
В подол собирали их в ночь грушепада.

Я — форма,
Я — корпус,
Я — цинковый конус.
Мое содержанье от формы свободно,
Мечами моркови и дынями полнюсь
И ломкою желтой ботвой огородной.

Я — форма. И люди царят надо мною,
Мое содержанье в меня собирая.
Когда ж не наполнена плотью земною,
Я небом, я небом налита до края.

The Ballad of the Pail

I'm a form out of zinc. I contain
Heavy pellets—the fruit of the dust-sprayed cherry.
Crimson sunsets and dawns they retain.
Now they doze in me, berry on berry.

I'm a form. In the autumn my content are pears,
The lamps of the orchard, the sun's gleaming rivals,
Stray souls of the bark-clad Republic of Sap
Gathered in aprons as welcome arrivals.

I'm a form.
I'm a body,
A cone out of zinc
Whose content is multiform—free of its form.
Filled with dagger-like carrots or beet to the brink
Or brittle green stalks, without measure or norm.

I'm a form. It's to man that I owe my birth
And what I am filled with is subject to him.
And when I am free of the flesh of the earth
I am laden with air full of sky to the brim.

Translated by Dorian Rottenberg

Yevgeni Yevtushenko (b. 1933) is a leader among modern Soviet poets. He is especially popular with students and young people. Yevtushenko's poetry is imbued with a sense of civic responsibility, it is publicistic in character, and constantly focused on the main problems of the day. At the same time it has the lyrical quality of an infinitely sincere confession. Yevtushenko travels a great deal, and has been to many countries in Europe, Asia and both North and South America. The bourgeois press at one time linked his youthful revolt against rigid dogmas with the mutiny of the Angry Young Men in the West. Yevtushenko himself has refuted this comparison. He is a consistent and ardent champion of revolutionary ideas and principles. An innovator in his own right, he develops certain of Mayakovsky's techniques especially as regards assonant rhyming.

YEVGENI YEVTUSHENKO

ЕВГЕНИЙ ЕВТУШЕНКО

М. Бернесу

Хотят ли русские войны?
Спросите вы у тишины
над ширью пашен и полей,
и у берез и тополей.
Спросите вы у тех солдат,
что под березами лежат,
и пусть вам скажут их сыны,
хотят ли русские войны.
Не только за свою страну
солдаты гибли в ту войну,
а чтобы люди всей земли
спокойно видеть сны могли.
Под шелест листьев и афиш
ты спишь, Нью-Йорк, ты спишь, Париж
Пусть вам ответят ваши сны.
хотят ли русские войны.
Да, мы умеем воевать,
но не хотим, чтобы опять
солдаты падали в бою
на землю грустную свою.
Спросите вы у матерей.
Спросите у жены моей.
И вы тогда понять должны,
хотят ли русские войны.

Do the Russians Want a War?

To Mark Bernes

Say, do the Russians want a war?—
Go ask our land, then ask once more
That silence lingering in the air
Above the birch and poplar there.
Beneath those trees lie soldier lads
Whose sons will answer for their dads.
To add to what you learned before,
Say—Do the Russians want a war?

Those soldiers died on every hand
Not only for their own dear land,
But so the world at night could sleep
And never have to wake and weep.
New York and Paris spend their nights
Asleep beneath the leaves and lights.
The answer's in their dreams, be sure.
Say—Do the Russians want a war?

Sure, we know how to fight a war,
But we don't want to see once more
The soldiers falling all around,
Their countryside a battleground.
Ask those who give the soldiers life,
Go ask my mother, ask my wife,
Then you will have to ask no more,
Say—Do the Russians want a war?

Translated by Tom Botting

Сопливый фашизм*

Финляндия,
           страна утесов,
                        чаек,
туманов,
        лесорубов,
                   рыбаков,
забуду ли,
          как, наш корабль встречая,
искрилась пристань всплесками платков,
как мощно пела молодость над молом,
как мы сходили в толкотне людской
и жали руки,
            пахнущие морем,
автолом
       и смоленою пенькой!..
Плохих народов нет.
                   Но без пощады
я вам скажу,
            хозяев не виня:
у каждого народа —
                  свои гады.
Так я про гадов.
               Слушайте меня.

---

* Стихотворение написано в связи с провокацион
  ными выступлениями правых сил на VIII Все
  мирном фестивале молодежи и студентов в Хель
  синки в 1962 году.

178

Snivelling Fascism*

Finland,
  country of seagulls
      and cliffs,
fishermen,
  timbermen,
     stoney earth!
Shall I ever forget,
   how,
     greeting our ship,
the landing-stage sparkled
     with a handkerchief surf,
how strong
   rang the song of the young
       as we
passed through the welcoming crowd,
      row by row
shaking strong hands,
    that smelt of the sea,
car-grease
   and well-tarred tow!
There are no bad nations.
     But without false mercy
I'll tell you—
   no blame on my hosts—
every nation
   has its own vermin.
So I'll talk about vermin.
     Here goes.

* The poem was written after provocative right-wing manifesta-
tions at the VIII World Youth Festival of Helsinki in 1962.

179

Пускай меня простят за это финны,
как надо называть,

все назову.
Фашизм я знал по книгам и по фильмам,
а тут его увидел наяву.
Фашизм стоял,

дыша в лицо мне виски,
у бронзовой скульптуры Кузнецов.
Орала и металась в пьяном визге
орава разгулявшихся юнцов.
Фашизму фляжки подбавляли бодрости.
Фашизм жевал с прищелком чуингам,
швыряя в фестивальные автобусы
бутылки,

камни
под свистки и гам.
Фашизм труслив был в этой стадной

наглости
Он был соплив,

прыщав
и белобрыс.
Он чуть не лез от ненависти на стену
и под плащами прятал дохлых крыс.
Взлохмаченный,

слюнявый,

мокролицый,
хватал девчонок,

пер со всех сторон
и улюлюкал ганцам и малийцам,
французам,

немцам,

да и финнам он.
Он похвалялся показною доблестью,
а сам боялся где-то в глубине

I hope
        I'll be forgiven by Finns
for calling a spade
                    a spade.
I'd learnt about fascism
                    from books and films
but here
        I saw it alive,
                    in full play.
It stood,
        breathing whiskey
                    into my face,
fascism,
        near the Blacksmiths' statue,
drunken yells
            all over the place
flying
        like clots of spittle
                    at you.
They swigged new courage
                    from whiskey flasks,
munched chewing gum
                with demented gusto,
hurled empty bottles
                    and stones at us
as we drove by
            in festival buses.
Yet they feared us,
                for all their wolf-pack
                                    audacity
the snivelling,
            warty,
                    dirty beasts,
their hatred switched on
                    to full capacity,
hiding dead rats
                their raincoats beneath.
The drooling,
            unkempt
                    and sweat-faced ruffians
grabbed at girls,
            lunged about
                            with a hullabaloo,
jeering
        at Malis
            and Ghanaians,
at Frenchmen,
            at Germans,
                        at you, Finns, too,
howling,
        their would-be prowess flaunting,
hiding
        how much they were really afraid,

и в рок-н-ролле или твисте дергался

с приемничком,

висящим на ремне.

Эх, кузнецы,

ну что же вы безмолвствовали?!

Скажу по чести —

мне вас было жаль.

Вы подняли бы

бронзовые молоты

и разнесли бы в клочья эту шваль!

Бесились,

выли,

лезли вон из кожи,

на свой народ пытаясь бросить тень...

Сказали мне —

поминки по усопшим

Финляндия справляет в этот день.

Но в этих подлецах,

пусть даже юных,

в слюне их истерических речей

передо мною ожил «Гитлерюгенд» —

известные всем ясли палачей.

«Хайль Гитлер!» —

в крике слышалось истошном

Так вот кто их родимые отцы!

Так вот поминки по каким усопшим

хотели справить эти молодцы!

Но не забыть,

как твердо,

угловато

у клуба «Спутник» —

прямо грудь на грудь —

стеною встали русские ребята,

как их отцы,

закрыв фашизму путь.

«Но — фестиваль!» —

взвивался вой шпанья,

with rock-n-roll
                        and twist contorting,
girt with transistors,
                        U.S.-made.
Now, Blacksmiths,
                        tell me,
                                why were you silent?
The hoodlums raged on,
                        but you kept mum:
you ought to have lifted
                        your great bronze hammer
and hammered them flat,
                        the fascist scum.
They ranted and raved
                        all decorum scorning,
dead-set
        to bring shame
                        on their nation's head.
I'm told,
        all Finland
                        that day was mourning
in sad solemnity
                        for her dead.
But in those scoundrels,
                        though only lads,
came alive
            the Hitlerjugend of old
the well-known butchers' créche
                        which our dads
had taught a lesson
                        worth its weight in gold.
"Heil Hitler!"
            echoed in their drunken yells.
So that's who they honoured
                        on Remembrance Day
We know
        who their ancestors were
                        jolly well,
a marvellous lineage,
                I must say.
Yet I'll never forget, too,
                how firmly stood
our Russian boys,
            to their fathers true,
at the Sputnik club
            resolved to stay put,
not to let
        the shadow of fascism through.
"No—festival!"
                rose
                    the hoodlums' roar.

«Но — коммунизм!» —
        был дикий рев неистов
И если б коммунистом не был я,
то в эту ночь
        я стал бы коммунистом!

"No—Communism!"
                    came the outcry
                                    dirty.
I swear,
        if I hadn't done so before,
that night
            I'd have joined the Party,
                                    for certain!

Translated by Dorian Rottenberg

Зависть

Завидую я.

        Этого секрета

не раскрывал я раньше никому.

Я знаю,

        что живет мальчишка где-то,

и очень я завидую ему.

Завидую тому,

        как он дерется, —

я не был так бесхитростен и смел.

Завидую тому,

        как он смеется, —

я так смеяться в детстве не умел.

Он вечно ходит в ссадинах и шишках —

я был всегда причесанней,

           целей.

Все те места,

        что пропускал я в книжках

он не пропустит.

        Он и тут сильней.

Он будет честен жесткой прямотою,

злу не прощая за его добро.

и там, где я перо бросал:

        «Не стоит...» —

он скажет:

    «Стоит!» —

        и возьмет перо.

Envy

I'm full of envy.
                        It's a truth I never
Disclosed before.
                        Yes, call it just a whim.
There lives a boy some place—
                        My friend? My
                                neighbour?
No.... I don't know him
                        but I envy him.
I like the daring way he fights his battles;
I was more   strait-laced, less naively bold.
I like his laugh, so unrestrained, so artless;
Mine was less childlike, if the truth be told.
My hair was plastered neatly—
                                his is tousled;
My knees were pink—
                        his knees are black and blue.
In books,
        I skipped the parts
                        that bored or puzzled—
He never does;
            he reads them.... reads them through.
Towards evil unforgiving, he will brusquely
Dismiss its righteous words.
                        Whereas I may
Throw down my pen: "It doesn't pay, too risky,"—
He'll pick up his.
                "It does!" he'll calmly say.

Он, если не развяжет,

                  так разрубит,

где я ни развяжу,

              ни разрублю.

Он, если уж полюбит,

                  не разлюбит,

а я и полюблю,

           да разлюблю.

Я скрою зависть.

            Буду улыбаться.

Я притворюсь, как будто я простак:

«Кому-то же ведь надо улыбаться,

кому-то же ведь надо жить не так...»

Но сколько б ни внушал себе я это,

твердя:

        «Судьба у каждого своя...»,

мне не забыть, что есть мальчишка где-то

что он добьется большего, чем я.

A knot he can't untie, he'll cut;

                  whilst striving

To do the same, I cannot hope to win.

I know that, once in love,

                he'll not stop loving,

While I keep falling out of love and in.

I'll mask my envy.

              I will smile, pretending

To be more guileless than I really am,

And say in tones remotely condescending,

"Not all of us can hope to be the same."

But all my words, I know, sound lame and empty

I can't forget, no matter how I try,

That there's a boy right in this very city,

A boy who will achieve

               much more than I.

Translated by Irina Zheleznova

Nikolai Zabolotsky (1903-1958) was a major Soviet poet. Fame came to him with the publication of his book of verse entitled "Columns" (1929). The main theme of Zabolotsky's poetry is Nature and its ties with Man, approached from a philosophical point of view. At first (until the 1930s) he seemed most strongly aware of the destructive character of Nature, perceiving it in a pantheistic and mythological light. Then a new theme appeared: reason bringing harmony into the sanguinary contradictions of blind Nature. In the middle of the 1950s (his best poems of this period are "Peasant Spokesmen", "The Opposition of Mars", "The Ugly Girl" and "Last Love") Zabolotsky turned to socio-psychological problems and strove for classic lucidity and better balanced imagery. His Russian translations of Georgian poetry also earned him high praise.

NIKOLAI ZABOLOTSKY

НИКОЛАЙ ЗАБОЛОЦКИЙ

Ходоки

В зипунах домашнего покроя,
Из далеких сел, из-за Оки,
Шли они, неведомые, трое —
По мирскому делу ходоки.

Русь металась в голоде и буре,
Всё смешалось, сдвинутое враз.
Гул вокзалов, крик в комендатуре
Человечье горе без прикрас.

Только эти трое почему-то
Выделялись в скопище людей,
Не кричали бешено и люто,
Не ломали строй очередей.

Всматриваясь старыми глазами
В то, что здесь наделала нужда,
Горевали путники, а сами
Говорили мало, как всегда.

Есть черта, присущая народу:
Мыслит он не разумом одним, —
Всю свою душевную природу
Наши люди связывают с ним.

Оттого прекрасны наши сказки,
Наши песни, сложенные в лад.
В них и ум и сердце без опаски
На одном наречьи говорят.

Peasant Spokesmen

In sheepskin coats of homely peasant cut
From villages far south of the Oka
They came, three strangers. Each had left his hut
To put his case about the way things are.

All Russia tossed, distraught by war and famine
With everything confused, disturbed, displaced.
She roared and argued, trains and stations cramming
With human misery, unhidden, open-faced.

Only those three strangers waited mildly
In a crowd that craved for bread and news,
Neither shouting frenziedly and wildly,
Nor upsetting order in the queues.

On the havoc born of need and hunger
Looked three pairs of travel-tired old eyes;
Sorrowful they stood there, lost in wonder,
Saying almost nothing, peasantwise.

There's a trait I treasure in my people:
They never reason with the mind alone,
But their hearts, too, are involved so deeply
That thought and feeling mingle into one.

That is why our folktales are so splendid,
So sincere and sensitive our songs
In that all-expressive language rendered
That to heart and mind alike belongs.

Эти трое мало говорили.
Что слова! Была не в этом суть.
Но зато в душе они скопили
Многое за долгий этот путь.

Потому, быть может, и таились
В их глазах тревожные огни
В поздний час, когда остановились
У порога Смольного они.

Но когда радушный их хозяин,
Человек в потертом пиджаке,
Сам работой до смерти измаян,
С ними говорил накоротке,

Говорил о скудном их районе,
Говорил о той поре, когда
Выйдут электрические кони
На поля народного труда,

Говорил, как жизнь расправит крылья
Как, воспрянув духом, весь народ
Золотые хлебы изобилья
По стране. ликуя, понесет, —

Лишь тогда тяжелая тревога
В трех сердцах растаяла, как сон,
И внезапно видно стало много
Из того, что видел только он.

И котомки сами развязались,
Серой пылью в комнате пыля,
И в руках стыдливо показались
Черствые ржапые крендедя.

С этим угощеньем безыскусным
К Ленину крестьяне подошли.
Ели все. И горьким был и вкусным
Скудный дар истерзанной земли.

Though little spoke the three, their hearts were
                                              burning.
What are words? Real truth is past their power.
All that they had felt upon their journey
Was hidden in their breasts until its hour.

Maybe that was why an anxious flicker
Came into the eyes on faces white
When they stopped, their heartbeats getting quicker,
At the gates of Smolny late at night.

But when their host, a man of over fifty
In a well-worn suit of darkish grey,
Tired to death himself with work and worry,
Addressed them in his simple, kindly way,

Talked about their famine-ridden village
And about the none-too-distant time
When an iron horse would do the tillage
And of how the yields would start to climb.

How life would flourish, filled with man-made
                                              wonders
And the people, happy in their hearts,
Would reap the golden harvest of abundance,
Gladness lighting up their native parts—

Only then the heavy, anxious feeling
Vanished from the bosoms of the three
And suddenly they too began discerning
Much that he alone till then could see.

And their knapsacks got undone as if by magic
Powdering the floor around with dust
And out of them too tasty to imagine—
Come home-baked krendels, little else but crust.

And they treated Lenin with those dainties
Offered with a humble, open hand.
Everybody ate. 'Twas sweet and bitter,
The meagre fruit of the tormented land.

Translated by Dorian Rottenberg

Некрасивая девочка

Среди других играющих детей
Она напоминает лягушонка.
Заправлена в трусы худая рубашонка,
Колечки рыжеватые кудрей
Рассыпаны, рот длинен, зубки кривы,
Черты лица остры и некрасивы.
Двум мальчуганам, сверстникам её,
Отцы купили по велосипеду.
Сегодня мальчики, не торопясь,
                                к обеду,
Гоняют по двору, забывши про неё,
Она ж за ними бегает по следу.
Чужая радость так же, как своя,
Томит ее и вон из сердца рвется,
И девочка ликует и смеется,
Охваченная счастьем бытия.

Ни тени зависти, ни умысла худого
Еще не знает это существо.
Ей всё на свете так безмерно ново,
Так живо всё, что для иных мертво!
И не хочу я думать, наблюдая,
Что будет день, когда она, рыдая,
Увидит с ужасом, что посреди подруг
Она всего лишь бедная дурнушка!
Мне верить хочется, что сердце не
                                        игрушка
Сломать его едва ли можно вдруг!

196

The Ugly Girl

The sparse, untidy, ginger-coloured curls
In meagre whisps about her head lie scattered;
Her little blouse is faded, old and tattered.
She looks a freak among the boys and girls
Playing around her, poor, misshapen creature
With crooked teeth and sharp, ungainly features
Not far away two handsome little lads
Enjoy the bicycles just bought them by their
                                        dads.
They ride about with happy turns and twists,
While she runs after, happy as the boys,
Though they are scarce aware that she exists.
Her heart is filled with other children's joys,
She laughs, their thoughtlessness forgiving,
An ugly little urchin with shrill voice,
In raptures at the sheer delight of living.

No shade of spite nor any evil notion
Has ever found its way into her head.
All in the world arouses her emotion,
All is alive to her which some of us think dead
And as I look I try to quench the fear
That there must come a day, perhaps quite near,
When all her ugliness the child at last will
                                        know,
And life for her will be deprived of joy,
I would not think the heart is just a toy
That can be broken by a single blow;

Мне верить хочется, что чистый этот пламень
Который в глубине ее горит,
Всю боль свою один переболит
И перетопит самый тяжкий камень!

И пусть черты ее нехороши
И нечем ей прельстить воображенье, —
Младенческая грация души
Уже сквозит в любом ее движенье.
А если это так, то что есть красота
И почему ее обожествляют люди?
Сосуд она, в котором пустота,
Или огонь, мерцающий в сосуде?

I still would hope that the unblemished beacon
Which shines within her with such brilliant light,
Will overcome the pain and burn as bright,
Will brave the worst of storms and never weaken.

Perhaps there is no beauty in her face
To captivate a man's imagination,
And yet her soul is lit with such a grace
That fills each step with animation.
If she be ugly, what is beauty then?
Why is it worshipped everywhere by men?
Is all its value in the outward form,
Or is it something hidden, live and warm?

Translated by Dorian Rottenberg

Silva Kaputikyan (b. 1919) is an Armenian poetess who began to publish her works in 1933. She was educated at Yerevan University from which she graduated in 1941. In the last ten years a change has come into her poetry. Her earlier vision of the world was rather superficial and illustrative ("These Days", "On the Bank of the Zanga", and "My Own" published in the period 1945-55) but then she began to come into her own as a mature poet ("Lyric Verse", 1955; "Verses", 1959; "Reflection on the Crossroads", 1960; and others) tackling serious moral problems of the society around her.

SILVA KAPUTIKYAN

СИЛЬВА КАПУТИКЯН

Небрежно и щедро я жизнь прожила,
Подобно ребенку, подобно царице, —
Быть может, я слабою слишком была,
Быть может, я силою вправе гордиться.

Я верила смело, мне лгали подряд,
Но — вместо проклятья, — уверясь в обмане
Сама от него отвратила я взгляд,
Чтоб только не видеть его покаяний!

Не шла ни за кем я, смиреньем дыша,
Где б дверь запереть — отворяла я двери.
В гордыне своей не считала душа
Незримые беды свои и потери...

Где нужно держать — я твердила: «уйди!»
Где нужно вернуть — не бежала вдогонку.
Беспечно теряла находки свои.
Где тихо бы плакать, смеялась я звонко.

Небрежно и щедро я жизнь прожила,
Подобно ребенку, подобно царице, —
Быть может, я слабою слишком была,
Быть может, я силою вправе гордиться...

Impulsive and lavish I lived all my days,
A childish, princesses' unthinking existence.
Perhaps I should feel I was weak in my ways,
Or maybe feel pride in my strength and consistence.

I trusted unwisely and listened to lies.
On sensing a falsehood, not blaming, nor ranting,
I turned in disgust and averted my eyes
For fear of the sight of deception recanting.

When doors should be closed, I would fling the doors
                                                wide.
In nobody's wake would I walk with breath bated.
All losses and ills by my soul, in its pride,
Remained unperceived and as evils not rated.

I always said "Go!" when I should have said "Stay!"
I never thought anyone worth running after,
And all that I found I would soon throw away.
I should have wept softly, but burst into laughter.

Impulsive and lavish I lived all my days,
A childish, princesses' unthinking existence.
Perhaps I should feel I was weak in my ways,
Or maybe feel pride in my strength and consistence.

Translated by Tom Botting

В Севанских горах

Купаясь в струях света, одиноко
Стояла я в тиши севанских круч.
Стояла я высоко, так высоко,

Что плеч моих орел крылом касался,
А ноги обвивало дымом туч.
Каким огромным, гордым мир казался!

Но вдруг, забыв о вековом просторе,
Я посмотрела вниз, ища жилья,
Ища тропинки на кремнистом взгорье.

По человеку стосковалась я!..

Among Sevan's Mountains

Among Sevan's steep mountains, stark and soundless,
I stood alone, in streams of light I bathed
And stood on high, until the heights seemed boundless

And eagles brushed my back with spreading pinion,
While round my legs the whispy clouds were swathed.
How huge the earth then seemed in proud dominion!

A sudden urge—forgetting ageless spaces—
I dropped my gaze to seek some path that ran
Among the rocky waste to dwelling places,

For deep within my heart I longed for Man...!

Translated by Tom Botting

205

Песня дорог

Как хорошо порой покинуть
И дом и город свой родной
И в мир, что пред тобой
                                        раскинут,
Отправиться совсем одной!
Где на земле еще дороги
Так бесконечно хороши?
Где ветер странствий и тревоги
Так освежающ для души?

Свободной красотой земною
Душа счастливая горда,
Когда мелькают пред тобою
Бесчисленные города.
Ни с кем из встречных не знакома
Идешь как будто бы одна,
Но знаешь, что и здесь ты дома,
В семью большую включена.

Пусть иногда меня не знают,
Откуда я, иду куда, —
Но незнакомую встречают
Гостеприимством города.
Как хорошо в краю далеком
По новым улицам пройти
И в лицах, что глядят из окон,
Родное, близкое найти!

Song of the Way

How good at times to leave the places,
The house, the town, that saw your birth
And over roads through unknown spaces
To walk alone upon our earth.
What other land has paths unending
Where always lovely scenes unroll?
What restless winds forever wending
Can bring such freshness to the soul?

Unfettered earthly beauty flashing
Inspires the heart with joy and pride
As past you countless towns go dashing
When down some far-off road you ride.
Although you seem alone, not meeting
A soul you know throughout the day,
You're sure there waits a friendly
                                    greeting
From your great family on the way.

Sometimes the people do not know me,
Where I shall go, or where I've been.
Yet generous towns a welcome show me—
A passer-by they'd never seen.
How good to walk in distant places,
Through streets where every house is new,
And in the windows notice faces
That seem so near and dear to you.

И сблизиться со всеми, зная,
Что здесь везде твоя семья
И что везде ты как родная,
И со своими и своя,
Где сразу станешь близкой всем ты
Увидишь столько доброты,
Когда хоть робко, хоть с акцентом
Заговоришь по-русски ты.

Как хорошо, душою доброй
Вобрав всей Родины простор,
Вернуться освеженной, бодрой
К подножью белоснежных гор,
Войти к друзьям и с жаждой новой
Вино своих садов испить
И под родимым кровом снова
Трудиться, радоваться, жить!..

Then being drawn to those around you,
And feeling kinship deep and warm,
You know these ties have always bound you
Since you and they one family form;
You're one of them, there's no discussion,
They'll show such kindness when you start
To speak in rather halting Russian
That you will guess you've won their heart.

How good it is, upon returning
From travelling through our mighty land,
To sense fresh force within you burning
And see the snow-capped range at hand;
To visit friends and find much stronger
The thirst for wines our gardens give
And in your home that waits no longer
To work rejoicing and—to live!

Translated by Tom Botting

Semyon Kirsanov (b. 1906) is an ardent propagandist of Mayakovsky with whom he was friends. Kirsanov's earlier poetry—the books "Aim" (1926), "Experiments" (1927) and "My Birthday Song" (1928)—bear evidence of his formalistic experimenting with words. In the 1930s he enthusiastically advocated the principles of "leftist" art, being a member of LEF, as this literary group was called, and fully supported publicist poetry based on facts and newspaper material. Still, his most important works—"Cinderella" (1936), "Your Poem" (1937) and "Seven Days of the Week" (1956) are lyrical in mood, and in them facts and naturalistic descriptions play a less important role than symbols and allegory. The chief characteristics of the work of this poet, who extols the omnipotence of the intellect, are the virtuosity in his use of words, the ingenuity of his plots, and the chiselled polish of the structure of his poems.

SEMYON KIRSANOV

СЕМЕН КИРСАНОВ

Этот мир

Мой родной, мой земной,
    мой кружащийся шар!
Солнце в жарких руках,
    наклонясь, как гончар,

вертит влажную глину,
    с любовью лепя,
округляя, лаская,
    рождая тебя.

Керамической печью
    космических бурь
обжигает бока
    и наводит глазурь,

наливает в тебя
    голубые моря,
и, где надо, — закат,
    и, где надо, — заря.

И когда ты отделан
    и весь обожжен —
Солнце чудо свое
    обмывает дождем

и отходит за воздух
    и за облака
посмотреть на творение
    издалека.

This World

My own planet, my Earth,
    My globe spinning through space!
By the sun's flaming hands
    You were launched on your race.

On his wheel your moist clay
    He lovingly threw
And with tender caresses
    Gave life unto you.

In the kilns of the cosmos
    Where cosmic storms blaze
You were fired and were tempered
    And coated with glaze.

When at last you were finished
    And fired, shining new,
The sun poured the oceans
    And seas onto you.

With dawns and with sunsets
    He painted you too,
Then washed you with showers
    He sent from the blue

O'er the firmament wide
    He then stepped aside,
Looked down on his masterpiece,
    Beaming with pride.

Ни отнять, ни прибавить
        такая краса!
До чего ж этот шар
        гончару удался!

Он, руками лучей
        сквозь туманы светя
дарит нам свое чудо:
        — Бери, мол, дитя,

дорожи, не разбей —
        на гончарном кругу
я удачи такой
        повторить не смогу!

For that globe was just perfect,
    No more and no less
And the potter was happy
    At such a success.

Through distant mists shining
    On the planet he smiled,
Then gave it to Man,
    Saying: "Take it, my child!

"Take care not to break it,
    For surely, I feel,
I'll never repeat it
    On my potter's wheel!"

Translated by Louis Zellikoff

Часы

Я думал, что часы — одни.
А оказалось,
                что они
и капельки, и океаны,
и карлики, и великаны.

И есть ничтожные века,
ничтожней малого мирка,
тысячелетья-
              лилипуты...

Но есть
        великие минуты,
И только ими ценен век,
и ими вечен человек,
и возмещают
              в полной мере
все дни пустые, все потери.

Я знал такие. Я любил.
И ни секунды не забыл!
Секунды —
          в мир величиною,
за жизнь изведанные мною!

И разве кончилось Вчера,
когда Ильич сказал: — Пора

Hours

All hours once seemed the same to me.
But it appears
         that they can be
Like tiny droplets and like seas,
Like mighty mountains and like fleas.

Some ages leave no trace behind
By which to be recalled to mind;
Millenniums—
         Lilliputian midgets...

There also are
         grand, glorious minutes—
By them alone an age is prized
And men—by them immortalised,
In which we find
         full compensation
For empty days, for all frustration.

These I knew too, when I drank love's
         fill
Each second I remember still;
Worlds in themselves, they will extend
Throughout my life until its end!

That great moment will ever last
When Lenin said: "The die is cast"?

Нет!
   Время Ленина
                все шире
жизнь озаряет в этом мире.

И так повсюду.
                Знает мир
часы карманов и квартир
и те — без никаких кронштейнов —
часы Шекспиров,
                часы Эйнштейнов!

Yes,

Lenin's time spreads ever wider
Across our life—no sunlight brighter.

Thus in all things.

We measure time
By clocks that tick and clocks that chime,
But how to measure all the ages,
That will be lived

by Shakespeare's pages?

Translated by Louis Zellikoff

David Kugultinov (b. 1922), a well-known Kalmyk poet, who was awarded the Russian Federation Literary Prize for 1967. His father was a schoolteacher. David Kugultinov had his first book "Poems of Youth" published in 1940, the year he completed his 10-year secondary education. That same year he was admitted to membership of the Union of Soviet Writers. He began the war as a private and then worked as a correspondent on his division's newspaper. After the war he graduated from the Literary Institute in Moscow. Since then David Kugultinov has published ten books in Kalmyk and Russian. His philosophical poetry treats the essence of eternal human values and concepts. Kugultinov's attitude to life and art is a firmly positive one: he is a genuinely modern poet, a man of courage and integrity. The main theme of his collections: "The Vision of the Heart", "The Sun's Equal", "I Am Your Contemporary", "To Earn a Friend's Love" and others, is Man and his attitude to the world around him, to people and to the problems of our times.

DAVID KUGULTINOV

ДАВИД КУГУЛЬТИНОВ

Мать-Родина!.. Так люди называли
Ее издревле... Вправду — не она ли
Нам жизнь дала, и силы в нас влила,
И за руку взяла и повела?..
Она щедра по-матерински, — знаю...
Но Родина — она и дочь родная.

Все лучшее — и труд и вдохновенье —
Самозабвенно отдаем мы ей,
Как только детям отдают — продленью
Быстротекущих, кратких наших дней...
Здесь все мое!.. Бери его, упрочь,
О Родина моя!.. О мать и дочь!

O Mother-Land! So people ever called her
From times of old... and truly, was it not her
Who gave us breath, and swelled our strength and health?
In hers our hands allied, became our guide?
Unstinting she, as mothers are—hereafter
Though Mother-Land... she yet is like a daughter.

And all the best—in work and inspiration—
Unselfishly, we give her in return,
As if to children—an extension
Of our swift-flowing, earthly short sojourn.
Here, all is mine!... But take it, grow, expand,
Sweet Mother, Daughter! You, my Mother-Land!

                              Translated by Gladys Evans

Когда давно желанные слова
Спешат ко мне, — окликну их едва;
Когда, в мой труд сегодня проникая
Отчетлив облик завтрашнего дня
И кажется, что вся судьба людская
Сейчас зависит только от меня, —
Событья обнажаются до корня,
Все тени исчезают на лету,
Все лица излучают доброту,
И все сердца становятся просторней
Тогда я нужен людям... И рука
Спешит за мыслью... И душа легка.

When those long-wished-for words rush to my mind
And in their proper sequence are alined,
When with my toil, Today I penetrate
And I Tomorrow's features clearly see,
And when it seems to me, Mankind's own fate
Just now depends on no one else but me—

The very root of things before me stands,
All shadows fly away to leave no trace,
And kindness radiates from every face,
And every heart with tenderness expands—
My people need me then ... as from a spring,
The thoughts flow from my pen ... my soul doth sing.

Translated by Louis Zellikoff

Когда иссякнут сил моих остатки,
И, вопреки рассудку,
                              вдруг,
Как конь, чей повод в вихре скачки
Наездник выронил из рук,
Любовь моя к тебе рванется,
И речь
Из родников мечты
Освобожденная польется, —
Не испугаешься ли ты?

Как прежде ли, не избегая,
Ты будешь другом звать меня?
Как прежде ль в тайны, дорогая,
Ты будешь посвящать меня?

И с детской радостью такою
В глаза доверчиво смотреть,
И руку маленькой рукою
Мне пожимать в минуты встреч?

...Не надо! Больше не могу!
Мне больно.
Прикованный к доверью твоему,
Кляня другого, делаюсь невольно
Сообщником твоей любви к нему.
И — как без слез порою плачут —
Ревную я
Без права и без слов...

When all my resolutions prove in vain
And, leaping over reason
                              in one flash,
Like some great steed whose rider dropped the rein
In sweeping whirlwind dash,
My love for you comes rearing, rushing
And words—
At last set free—
From the sources of my dreams rise gushing,
Will you not feel fear of me?

Will you be the same and greet me,
Call me friend, just as before?
And, my dear, each time you meet me
Will you bare your soul once more?

Will your smile be sweet, unworried,
And in your eyes will trust still shine?
With a gesture, calm, unhurried,
Will you place your hand in mine?

...No! No more! Stop! You must!
This pain is far beyond all bearing.
You have me shackled. It is not just!
For, hating him whose secrets I am sharing,
I accede to your love by accepting your trust.
As men can weep, yet no tears dim their sight,
My jealous heart
Is mute, deprived of right....

227

Прошу тебя:
С ним обо мне,
А не о нем со мною
Ты говори, любя иль не любя.
Не мать и не подруга я.
Иные
Ты мне слова и мысли приготовь
И не вверяй мне
Тайн своих отныне,
И дружбой
Не карай мою любовь.

Arkadi Kuleshov (b. 1914). This well-known Byelorussian poet was the son of a schoolteacher and himself studied at the Minsk Teachers' Training College. His first poetic work was published in 1936. The patriotic poems "Brigade Flag" (1942), "Cymbalon", "House No. 24" (1944) and the volume "Verses and Poems" (1962) won him wide popularity. A master of epic poetry, Kuleshov follows the tradition of psychological reflection. The style of his lyric verse is vividly metaphorical.

Arkadi Kuleshov is also known as a translator of poetry into Byelorussian; his translation of Pushkin's "Eugene Onegin", for instance, received high praise from the critics.

Hear my plea—
Do speak of me to him,
But not of him to me.
Whether or not you love another
I am no confidant, or mother.
I beg you—
Start to seek out other words than those
You used to show your inner heart.
Secrets in me do not repose
And friendship on love
No longer impose.

Translated by Tom Botting

ARKADI KULESHOV

АРКАДИЙ КУЛЕШОВ

Часы мои — не солнца диск в зените,
Не сердце, будоражащее грудь.
Вращаясь равномерно по орбите,
Сама земля мой измеряет путь.

Дней и ночей блюдя чередованье,
На месте не стоят материки.
На их живом, мелькающем экране
Видны дорог и речек рушники.

Ковры весны преобразятся в лето,
Круженье листопада — в первый снег,
Я не хочу, чтоб некогда все это
Хотя б на миг остановило бег.

Застынет сердце, солнце в тучах сгинет,
Но ты, Земля, вертись, чтоб мне помочь
Не дай упасть на темной половине,
Где дня не будет, будет только ночь!

My clock is not the sun that rides the skies
And not the heart that pulses in this breast.
My pace is measured by this steady Earth that flies
Along its orbit, never stopping for a rest.

Night follows day in regular succession
Above the continents resembling screens in motion
With roads and rivers like gay ribbons flashing
Across their face framed by the heaving ocean.

In time soft spring gives way to summer's grandeur,
The whirl of falling leaves—to sweeping snow.
I dread to think of all this coming to a standstill
If only for a moment—who can know?

This heart may freeze—this sun forever hide,
But you, my Earth, my last support, spin on!
Don't let me fall upon the darkened side
Where night will reign, daylight forever gone.

Translated by Dorian Rottenberg

Нет, звезд я не хватаю с небосклона,
В лугах не рву весенние цветы,
Чтоб от меня как дар души влюбленной
Их благосклонно принимала ты.

Пускай цветы пестреют на поляне,
Чтоб мы с тобой бродили среди них.
Они увянут к вечеру в стакане,
Как мы без солнца среди стен немых.

Путь к звездам долог — за тысячелетья
До них и резвый конь не довезет.
За ними бы помчался я в ракете,
Да поздно отправляться мне в полет.

Нагрузки сердце выдержать не сможет,
В груди заглохнуть мой мотор готов.
Глотал он пыль дорог и бездорожий,
Прими его без звезд и без цветов!

No, not for me to catch the stars above
Or pluck the springtime flowers in meadows fair
To carry them to you as gifts of love
To be accepted with a gracious air.

Let flowers remain ungathered in the glade
For us to roam among them arm in arm.
Put them in flowerbowls and by evening they will fade
The lack of air and sunshine does them harm.

The distance to the stars is far too great.
All I can do is watch them in the night.
A rocket might have helped—but it is late,
Too late for me to undertake the flight.

The strain would be too heavy for this heart,
An engine near the limit of its powers,
Clogged by the dust of countless roads and paths.
So take just it with neither stars nor flowers.

Translated by Dorian Rottenberg

Сравнить бы музу с матерью моей,
Но слов не нахожу я для сравнений.
Ведь мать одна, как солнце в день весенний
Она самой поэзии родней.

Сравнить я мог бы музу с первой тропкой,
Что песню обвела вокруг села,
Когда б меня с моею музой робкой
Дорогам тропка не передала.

Когда б из рук полей не передали
Меня проселки рельсовым путям,
А рельсы — новой, неоглядной дали.
Какое музе я сравненье дам?

Она моя судьба на белом свете,
С неугасимой жаждою в глазах:
Тропинки вслед за ней бегут, как дети,
Навстречу ей летит за шляхом шлях.

My muse—I would compare her with my mother
But what comparison between them can there be?
I had one mother and will never have another,
Dearer she is than even poetry to me.

I might compare my muse to the first path
Which started me towards the realm of verse,
If that first path had not led on to roads
That took me all across the universe.

Passing me on to motorways and rails,
That path fell long ago into disuse,
And I go on, led by a light that never fails.
Then what comparison is there to fit my muse?

She is my destiny that travels with mankind
With unabated longing in her eyes.
Path after path, road after road is left behind,
And new horizons endlessly arise.

Translated by Dorian Rottenberg

Круженье листопада в первый снег
Преобразится — все в природе рядом.
Я словно бы командую парадом
Двух вражьих сил у пограничных вех,
Сраженьем снегопада с листопадом.

Я — повелитель всех дорог и рек,
Регулировщик карусели этой,
Как будто не проносит над планетой
Меня листком, снежинкою, ракетой
Сквозь толщу атмосферы бурный век.

В круженье лет песчинкой на планете
Я был зерном и пылью на току.
Двадцатый век стареющий наметил
Мой крайний срок. Но назло старику
Природе руки протяну вот эти
Из нашего
                    в грядущее столетье.

The whirl of snow succeeds the whirl of leaves.
All things in nature come in ordered alternation.
1 seem to supervise the confrontation
Of hostile forces which a time-built frontier cleaves:
Of leaves and snow engaged in livelong altercation.

I am the lord of all the roads and streams,
The regulator of this whole merry-go-round,
Although I, too, am swept across the ground
Like leaves or snowflakes or a rocket Venus-bound,
Swept by Time's whirl beyond the sky's farthest extremes

These whirling years I'm like a particle ill-fated
Of sand, a grain of dust or wheat on threshing ground.
The aging twentieth century has dated
My time-limit. And yet, if only to confound
Fate, I'll extend these hands with unabated
Fervour to greet the Golden Age so long-awaited.

Translated by Dorian Rottenberg

Kaisyn Kuliev (b. 1917) is a native of Kabardino-Balkaria in the Caucasus. An exceptionally gifted lyric poet, he writes in the aphoristic, austerely reserved manner peculiar to Caucasian folk poetry. He writes of fortitude in the face of tribulation, staunchness of spirit, and on such simple universal themes as love, motherhood, and fidelity to one's duty. "The Wounded Stone" (1964), considered his best collection of recent years, has been awarded the Russian Federation State Prize.

In his latest book "Peace to Your House" (1966), Kaisyn Kuliev for the first time in his career used the traditional genre of Caucasian poetry—eight and twelve-line stanzas.

KAISYN KULIEV

КАЙСЫН КУЛИЕВ

Где-то стонет женщина вдали,
Напевает песню колыбельную.
Вечный страх, тревоги всей земли
Проникают в песню колыбельную.

Первой пулей на войне любой
Поражает сердце материнское.
Кто б ни выиграл последний бой,
Но страдает сердце материнское.

Far away a woman can be heard
Moaning as she croons a lullaby,
All the fears and worries of the world
Weave themselves into that lullaby.

Every bullet fired in a war
Finds its mark—a mother's heart.
And whoever victory may score,
There'll be broken mothers' hearts.

Translated by Olga Shartse

«Растет ребенок плача» — есть пословица
Но если плач ребенка слышу вдруг,
Так больно сердцу моему становится,
Как будто горы в трауре вокруг.

Я помню, как детей беда военная
Гнала в крови, средь выжженных путей.
Мне кажется: рыдает вся вселенная, —
Когда я слышу плачущих детей.

"When children cry, they grow," so people say.
But when I hear a youngster cry forlornly,
My heart turns over with such dreadful pain,
The very mountains round me seem to put on mourning

I can't forget those children in the burnt-out rye,
The gory flames of war upon them creeping...
And every time I hear a youngster cry
I fancy that the Universe is weeping.

Translated by Olga Shartse

Сожженной Хиросимы горький дым
Проник в мой дом, и я опять страдаю
И дым Освенцима ползет за ним.
Чернеет он, мне душу угнетая.

Земля — нам дом родной, единый дом.
Когда в нем праздник, я его участник,
Смеюсь, пляшу — все ходит ходуном,
Но если в нем несчастье, я несчастен.

Мы все — ограда дома. Силой всех
Он устоять способен в наше время.
Кто это сердцем понял — Человек:
Пить может из одной реки со всеми.

На праздниках твоих пляшу я всласть,
Дом, где я рос, — земля моя большая.
Но в день беды готов я мертвым пасть
Пасть, твой порог врагу не уступая.

The acrid smoke of Hiroshima
Has seeped into my home.

                      Again I feel involved.
The smoke of Auschwitz next seeps in,
And as it thickens,

                  anguish fills my soul.

Our land is home to us, our common home.
When there's a celebration on I dance with zest,
I laugh and sing, all's merriment and fun.
But when misfortune visits us, I am distressed.

We form the wall around this house,

                        and it can
In unity withstand and weather anything.
All those who feel it thus,

                deserve the name of Man,
And can imbibe with others from the common spring.

My home where I was reared! My land so fair!
At all your holidays I will be gay.
But in your hour of trial I'll be prepared
To die but keep the enemy away.

                    Translated by Olga Shartse

Женщина купается в реке

Женщина купается в реке,
Солнце замирает вдалеке,

Нежно положив на плечи ей
Руки золотых своих лучей.

Рядом с ней, касаясь головы,
Мокнет тень береговой листвы.

Затихают травы на лугу,
Камни мокрые на берегу.

Плещется купальщица в воде,
Нету зла, и смерти нет нигде.

В мире нет ни вьюги, ни зимы
Нет тюрьмы на свете, ни сумы

Войн ни на одном материке...
Женщина купается в реке.

A Woman's
Bathing in the Stream

A woman's bathing in the stream.
Bemused, the sun upon her beams,
And on her shoulders gently lays
The fingers of its golden rays.

The willows cast their shadows far
To touch the woman's face and arms.
The reeds look on in silence bound,
Nor do the pebbles make a sound.

There is no evil anywhere,
No death, no sorrow, no despair,
No storms, no winter any more.
No prison bars, no need, no war.

The world's at rest. Peace reigns supreme.
A woman's bathing in the stream.

Translated by Olga Shartse

Речь горцев не цветиста, а сурова,
Их разговор бесхитростен и прост
Настолько, что боюсь я вставить
                               слово,
Как конь боится выскочить на мост.

Здесь говорят, не повышая голос,
Неприхотлив крестьянский разговор,
Но слово совершенно, словно колос,
Бесхитростно, как каменный забор.

Тревожит рассуждающих не вечность,
Не старый спор: что истина, что прах?
И в речи их нет слова «человечность»,
А просто человечность в их словах.

Течет неприхотливая беседа,
Бывая только тем омрачена,
Что ночью телка пала у соседа,
Что нет кормов и далека весна.

И о насущном хлебе вновь заходит
Речь горских мудрецов, и речь
                                     сама
Родной землею пахнет и походит
На их нелегкий хлеб и на корма.

The speech of mountain people is not flowery, it's
                                                    stern.
Their conversation is so simple and abridged,
So artless that I fear to put a word in out of turn,
Just as a horse fears stepping off the road onto
                                                    a bridge

Their conversation is of social graces shorn.
The peasant talk is low in voice and tone.
But every word's as perfect as an ear of corn,
As simply chiselled and as solid as a wall of stone.

And in their talk they do not stop to muse
On age-old questions: what is truth, what vanity?
The word "humanity" as such they never use,
But everything they say bespeaks humanity.

The only things that can disturb the gentle flow
Is news that someone's heifer died the night before,
Or apprehension that the fodder's running low
And spring will not be come for a month or more.

The conversation of the mountain sages
Revolves round vital problems of the day,
Their very speech, unchanging through the ages,
As fragrant as their hard-earned bread and hay.

Я не вступаю в споры-разговоры,
Мне все равно, кто прав и кто не прав,
Мне сладко просто слышать речь, в которой
И доброта хлебов, и мудрость трав.

To join in their debates I don't make bold:
It matters not to me who's right, who's wrong.
I simply like to hear their speech that holds
The wisdom of the herbs, the kindliness of corn

Translated by Olga Shartse

Vladimir Lugovskoy (1901-1957) entered the literary scene at the same time as Selvinsky, Antokolsky, Tikhonov and Bagritsky. Originally he belonged to the constructivist group of poets and sought to express the wisdom of the revolution in a dry, matter-of-fact manner, using stark, precise formulae. In the 1930s Lugovskoy did a lot of travelling, discovering for himself the world of Central Asia and the Caucasus, which was then going through a turbulent process of revolutionary transformation.

The last years of Lugovskoy's life were marked by an extraordinary upsurge of creative energy. His philosophical epic "The Middle of the Century" comprising twenty-five lyric poems, his lyric collections "The Summer Equinox" and "Blue Spring" capture the reader's imagination with their wealth of ideas and their emotional force.

VLADIMIR LUGOVSKOY
ВЛАДИМИР ЛУГОВСКОЙ

Вступление

Из поэмы „СЕРЕДИНА ВЕКА"

Передо мною середина века.
Я много видел.

            Многого не видел.

Вокруг не понял и в себе не понял.
В душе не видел, на земле не видел.
И все ж пойми — вот исповедь моя:
Я был участником событий мощных
В истории людей. Что делать мне —
Простому сыну века?

           Говорить

О времени, о том неповторимом,
Единственном на свете. О гиганте,
Который поднялся над всей землей,
На плечи взяв судьбу и жизнь планеты.
Как единична жизнь!

           В мозгу людей

Миры летят и государства гибнут.
В ночном раздумье человека ходят
Народы по намеченным путям.
И все же ты лишь капля в океане
Истории народа.

           Но она —

В тебе. Ты — в ней. Ты за нее в ответе
За все в ответе — за победы, славу,
За муки и ошибки.

256

Introduction

To the poem THE MIDDLE OF THE CENTURY

I'm at the middle of the twentieth century.
I've seen a lot.

But much I did not see.
I missed so many things around and in me,
I failed to see them in my soul and in the
world.
Still, try to understand, here's my confession
I took a part in happenings tremendous
In human history.

What must I do,
Man from the ranks, an offspring of the age?
Speak of our times. Unique. Unprecedented.
Speak of the giant towering above the world
And on his mighty shoulders hoisting
The burden of the planet's life and fate.
How singular is life!

In people's minds
Whole worlds go toppling, countries perish,
And nations follow paths outlined for them
In men's nocturnal brooding thoughts,
And yet, you're just a drop of water in the
ocean
Of history.

But then this history's in you.
You're in it. And you're answerable for it.
For everything—for victories, for glory,
For anguish, for mistakes.

И за тех,
Кто вел тебя. За герб, и гимн, и знамя
Я уходил от виденья прямого.
Слепила слабость, принижала робость,
Мешала суетность, манила сладость
Земных ночей, звериное тепло.
Но, даже будь я зорок до конца,
Лишь малое сумел бы я увидеть.
Я спотыкался, падал, поднимался
И снова шел.
Увы, я не пророк.
Я лишь поэт, который славит время,
Живое, уплотненное до взрыва,
Великое для жизни всей земли.

Да, весь я твой, живое время, весь
До глуби сердца, до предсмертной
мысли.
И я горжусь, что вместе шел с тобой,
С тобой, в котором движущие силы —
Октябрь, Народ и Ленин, весь я в них.
Они внутри меня. Мы неразрывны.
И в том, что я сегодня записал,
Я слышу голоса, я вижу мысли
Других людей, друзей, живых и
мертвых.
Я записал все так, как я увидел,
И как умел, и как вообразил.
Я всюду вижу горькие пробелы —
Мне десять жизней нужно бы прожить,
Чтоб передать богатство нашей жизни,
То главное, что принесли мы в мир
На смену старому, в средину века.
Без сказки правды в мире не бывает.
Мне сказочное видится во всем:
В борьбе, природе, в жизни человека.
Я твой, живое время, весь я твой!

Я за окном услышал хруст шагов —
Идет румяный человек в ушанке.
Как молод он! Как щеки разгорелись
От холода! Журнал зажат под мышкой.

                                        and for the men
Who led you.

            For your flag, your emblem and your anthem
I know I shrank from squarely facing things.
My weakness blinded me, my shyness dwarfed.
The vanity of living, the allure of earthly joys,
Of purely carnal warmth held me too fast.
But even if I'd had the keenest vision
There's very little that I could have seen
I stumbled, fell, got back on to my feet,
And carried on.

            Alas, I am no prophet,
I'm just a poet who extols his times, his epoch,
That's packed to bursting point, alive and vital,
A time of great import for all the world of men.
My epoch, I belong to you with all my being,
I'm yours until my dying thought, all yours!
And I am proud that I was with you always,
With you, my time, whose motive forces were
The Revolution, Lenin, and the People.
I live by them. They live in me. We are as one.
And as I write these lines today I seem to hear
The voices and I seem to see the thoughts
Of others, friends, the living and the dead.

I've written everything the way I saw it,
The way I had imagined it, as best I could
It pains me now that I've left out so much,
But I would need ten lifetimes at the very least
To paint in words the richness of our life,
And that which we have brought into the world
In this mid-century to take the place of old.
There's always something fabulous about the truth
And I, I see the fabulous in everything:
In nature, and in struggle, and in life itself.
And I am yours, my epoch, yours completely!

I hear the crunch of footsteps of the snow   outside.
A man is walking past. How vigorous his stride!
How young! How red his cheeks, how bright his eyes!
He seems to scorn the cold, his coat's so light.
He's carrying a rolled-up magazine.

Пальто подбито ветром. Подожди,
Ты, молодость, ты, будущее наше!
Я здесь с тобой. Ты видишь эту книгу?
Я протянул ее.
                              Возьми ее!

Hello!
Hello, our youth. Hello, our future. Wait for me!
I'm here with you, I'm coming. See this book?
I hold it out to him.

Here, take it, it's for you.

Translated by Olga Shartse

Та, которую я знал

Нет,
    та, которую я знал,
                    не существует.
Она живет
        в высотном доме,
                    с добрым мужем
Он выстроил ей дачу, он ревнует,
Он рыжий перманент
               ее волос
                  целует.
Мне даже адрес,
        даже телефон ее
                  не нужен.
Ведь та,
      которую я знал,
                не существует.
А было так,
       что злое море
             в берег било,
Гремело глухо,
      туго,
           как восточный бубен.
Неслось
     к порогу дома,
            где она служила.
Тогда она
     меня
       так яростно любила.

The Woman I Had Known

The woman I had known
                    does not exist.
She shares a smart apartment
                    with her worthy husband,
He built a summer place for her,
                    he's jealous of his
                                        bliss,
Her permed and tinted hair
                    he loves to kiss.
I have no need of her address,
                    I will not write
                                        or call her
For, after all,
          the woman I had known
                    does not exist.
And yet,
          it all has been:
                    the angry, pounding surf,
That beat as hollowly and tautly
                    as an Eastern drum,
And rushed to lick the doorstep of that woman's
                                        home.
She loved me,
          violently,
                    fiercely then.

263

Твердила,
что мы ветром будем,
морем будем.
Ведь было так,
что злое море
в берег било.
Тогда на склонах
остролистник рос
колючий
И целый месяц
дождь метался
по гудрону.
Тогда
под каждой
с моря налетевшей
тучей
Нас с этой женщиной
сводил
нежданный случай
И был подобен свету,
песне, звону.
Ведь на откосах
остролистник рос
колючий.
Бедны мы были,
молоды,
я понимаю.
Питались
жесткими, как щепка,
пирожками.
И если б
я сказал тогда,
что умираю
Она
до ада бы дошла,
дошла до рая,
Чтоб душу друга
вырвать
жадными руками
Бедны мы были,
молоды —
я понимаю!
Но власть
над ближними
ее так грозно съела
Как подлый рак
живую ткань
съедает.
Все,
что в ее душе
рвалось, металось, пело, —

We'd be like wind
                     and sea,
                                   she promised me again,
                                                          again.
It's true,
          it all has been:
                                   the angry, pounding surf,
The hillsides
              with the prickly holly overrun,
The wind-borne rain
                         that poured a whole month long,
When under every raincloud,
                                  blotting out the sun,
We met,
        that woman and myself,
                                   at every turn.
And it was beautiful.
                          Like light,
                                     like ringing bells,
                                                      like song.
We two were poor and young.
                                  Of course, I understand.
We lived on stale old pies
                           which we thought tasted grand.
And if I'd told her then that I was soon to die
She would have moved both heaven and earth,
                                               and hell itself
                                                          defied
To hold on to my soul
                         with greedy, grasping hands.
We two were poor and young.
                                  Of course, I understand.
But then,
         her thirst for power over men became a morbid
                                                        germ,
An ugly cancer,
                 eating living cells away.
And everything that in her soul had sung and burned
Turned into flesh—
                   her body,
                                 beautiful and firm.

265

Все перешло
в красивое, тугое тело.
И даже
            бешеная прядь ее,
                        со школьных лет седая
От парикмахерских
                        прикрас
                            позолотела.
Та женщина
            живет
                с каким-то жадным горем.
Ей нужно
        брать
            все вещи,
                что судьба дарует,
Все принижать,
            рвать—
                и цветок и корень.
И ненавидеть
            мир
                за то, что он просторен.
Но в мире
        больше с ней
                мы страстью
                        не поспорим
Той женщине
            не быть
                ни ветром
                        и ни морем.
Ведь та,
        которую я знал,
                не. существует.

The hair I loved,
                    with its unruly strand of early grey,
Was dyed a brilliant golden-red
                              and tightly permed.
This woman's life is tense with greed
                              that's like despair:
Whatever there's to take
                    she feels that she must seize.
A flower if she picks,
                    the roots she does not spare,
She tramples all,
              she hates the world
                              for being free.
We have no cause to clash,
                    no passion left to share.
This woman will not ever be the wind,
                              nor yet the sea.
That other one,
              the one that I had known,
                              exists no more
                                        for me.

Translated by Olga Shartse

Фотограф

Фотограф печатает снимки.
Ночная, глухая пора.
Под месяцем, в облачной дымке
Курится большая гора.

Летают сухие снежинки,
Окончилось время дождей.
Фотограф печатает снимки —
Являются лица людей.

Они выплывают нежданно,
Как луны из пустоты.
Как будто со дна океана
Средь них появляешься ты.

Из ванночки, мокрой и черной,
Глядит молодое лицо.
Порывистый ветер нагорный
Листвой засыпает крыльцо.

Под лампой багровой хохочет
Лицо в закипевшей волне.
И вырваться в жизнь оно хочет
И хочет присниться во сне.

Скорее, скорее, скорее
Глазами плыви сквозь волну!
Тебя я дыханьем согрею,
Всей памятью к жизни верну.

Photographs

A photographer's busy printing
Some pictures he made long ago.
It's night. Just the new moon glinting
On the smoking mountain below.

Flakes of dry snow are flying,
The season of rains is done.
He's busy printing and drying,
And faces emerge one by one.

They seem to rise up from the ocean,
So strangely they come into view,
Like moons from the void in their motion
And suddenly—there is you.

Your face, insecure as a phantom,
Looks up from the little black bath.
A wind blowing down from the mountain
Strews leaves on the garden path...

The ruby light falls on the photo,
Your laughing face tilts up and gleams,
It wants to break free of the water,
It wants to come back in dreams.

Oh, hurry, rise up from the water,
And surface the wave with your eyes.
My breath will, I prómise you, warm you,
My memory'll bring you to life!

Но ты уже крепко застыла,
И замерла волн полоса.
И ты про меня позабыла —
Глядят неподвижно глаза.

Но столько на пленке хороших
Ушедших людей и живых,
Чей путь через смерть переброшен
Как линия рельс мостовых.

А жить так тревожно и сложно,
И жизнь не воротится вспять.
И ведь до конца невозможно
Дру́г дру́га на свете понять.

И люди, еще невидимки,
Торопят — фотограф, спеши!
Фотограф печатает снимки.
В редакции нет ни души.

But you have already hardened.
The ripple of water is still.
You must have forgotten about me—
Your look is so stony and chill.

The film holds so many others,
Good people—living or gone,
Who'll pass over death by this causeway,
And come back again from beyond.

But life is hard and demanding,
And you can't live it over again.
Alas, there is no understanding
Each other to the end...

The people still hidden from sight
Keep urging him on and on.
The newspaper office is closed for the night.
He's working there all alone.

Translated by Olga Shartse

Mikhail Lukonin (b. 1918) was born into a peasant family. After school he worked at a factory and then enrolled at the Literary Institute in Moscow. When the war with Germany broke out he joined up at once and the glory of the people's heroism is reflected in his first slim volume, entitled "Heartbeat", which came out in 1947.

His attitude to the role of art is akin to that of Mayakovsky, and his credo "to be in the thick of the epoch's events and happenings" lent his poetry its civic character. Mikhail Lukonin's most widely-read works are his poem "Declaration of Love", his cycles "Long Distance Poetry", "Testing for Rupture", "The Road to Peace", and his latest book "Overcoming".

MIKHAIL LUKONIN

МИХАИЛ ЛУКОНИН

Мои друзья

Госпиталь.
Все в белом.
Стены пахнут сыроватым мелом.
Запеленав нас туго в одеяла
И подтрунив над тем, как мы малы,
Нагнувшись, воду по полу гоняла
Сестра.

А мы глядели на полы.
И нам в глаза влетала синева,
Вода, полы.
Кружилась голова.
Слова кружились:

              — Друг, какое нынче?

                  Суббота?

           — Вот, не вижу двадцать дней
Пол голубой в воде, а воздух дымчат.
— Послушай, друг... —

              И все о ней, о ней...

Несли обед. Их с ложки всех кормили.
А я уже сидел спиной к стене.
И капли щей на одеяле стыли.
Завидует танкист ослепший мне
И говорит

        про то, как двадцать дней
Не видит. И —

           о ней, о ней, о ней...

My Friends

In hospital.
Whiteness is all.
Damply the whitewash smells on each wall.
Swaddling us tight in blankets once more
small as children, with jokes well-meant,
the nurse chased water across the floor.

And still at the floorboards gazing we lay
and into our eyes a deep blue spread,
floorboards, water....
Swirled every head,
all words went swirling.

"What day's today?"
"Saturday, why?"
"It's twenty days then since I went blind."
Light-blue the floor and the air a haze.
"Listen, my friend,
                              be happy about her. Your love won't
                                                                  end."

They brought our dinner. From spoons they were fed.
I sat up, pillow-propped, quietly,
while the soup-drops chilled on the blanketed bed
and the eyeless tankman who envied me
talked of his sight
                              twenty days gone,
and talked of his girl,
                              talked on and on.

275

— А вот сестра,

                    ты письма продиктуй ей.
— Она не сможет, друг,

                            тут сложность есть...
— Какая сложность? Ты о ней не думай.
— Вот ты бы взялся!

                    — Я?...

                            — Ведь руки есть?

— Я не смогу!

                — Ты сможешь!..

                            — Слов не знаю

— Я дам слова!

                — Я не любил...

                            — Люби!..

Я научу тебя, припоминая...
Я взял перо.

                А он сказал: — «Родная!»
Я записал. Он:

                — «Думай, что убит...» —
«Живу», — я написал. Он:

                            — «Ждать не надо...»
А я, у правды всей на поводу,
Водил пером: «Дождись, моя награда!..»
Он: — «Не вернусь...»
А я: «Приду!.. Приду!..»

Шли письма от нее. Он пел и плакал,
Письмо держал у просветленных глаз.
Теперь меня просила вся палата:
— Пиши!..

                Их мог обидеть мой отказ.
— Пиши!..

            — Но ты же сам сумеешь, левой!
— Пиши!..

            — Но ты же видишь сам?!

Все в белом.
Стены пахнут сыроватым мелом,
Где это все? Ни звука. Ни души.
Друзья, где вы?..

"See,.here's the nurse,
                    she'll take down your letter."
"No, there's a problem,
                    friend, understand."
"What problem? Don't mind her,
                            who could be better?"
"If only you...."
                "I?"
                        "Well, haven't you hands?"
"But I can't."
                "That's not so."
                            "The words won't be right
"I'll tell them."
                    "I've never yet loved...."
                                    "Then it's
                                        time:
I'll tell you the way, I'll remember. Now write."
I took up the pen and he told me, "My own."
I wrote it. He added,
                "Consider me dead."
"I'm alive," I wrote, and he said,
                        "Don't expect me."
And I, in the cause of the whole truth, wrote down,
"Expect me, my darling, directly."
He said, "Won't return."
                        I wrote, "Coming soon."

Her letters answered, he sang and he wept.
He held her letters to eyes with no light.
Now the whole ward kept pleading with me:
"Write!"
        A refusal would sound a sad slight.
"Write."
        "You could write it yourself with your left.'
"Write!"
        "You can see: why not do it?"
                            "You write!"

Whiteness is all.
Damply the whitewash smells on each wall.
Where has it gone? Not a soul, not a sound.
Friends, where are you?

Светает у причала.
Вот мой сосед дежурит у руля.
Все в памяти переберу сначала.
Друзей моих ведет ко мне земля.
Один мотор заводит на заставе,
Другой с утра пускает жернова.
А я?
А я молчать уже не вправе,
Порученные мне горят слова.
— Пиши! — диктуют мне они.

                    Сквозная
Летит строка.
— Пиши о нас! Труби!..
— Я не смогу!
          — Ты сможешь!
                        — Слов не знаю
— Я дам слова!
          Ты только жизнь люби!

The dawn breaks over the mooring-place.
I'm homing. The helmsman beside me stands.

In memory all from the outset I trace.
The land slides closer, bringing old friends.
At the gates of the lock a motor now starts;
an engine's been driving the millworks for long.
And I—
   I know that my silence is wrong.
The words I've been trusted with burn in my heart.
"Write," they dictate.
      The line leaps in my mind.
"Write about us,
    cry out till all heed."
"I can't."
   "But you can."
       "What right words can I find?"
"I'll tell you.
    Love life, and that's all that you need."

Translated by Jack Lindsay

Нет памяти у счастья.

         Просто нету.

Я проверял недавно

И давно.

Любая боль оставит сразу мету,

А счастье — нет.

Беспамятно оно.

Оно как воздух — чувствуем и знаем,

Естественно, как воздух и вода.

Вот почему

И не запоминаем,

И к бедам не готовы никогда.

О счастье

Говорить —

И то излишне.

Как сердце — полагается в груди,

Пока не стиснет боль, оно неслышно

И кажется —

Столетья впереди.

Удивлена ты:

              я смеюсь, не плачу.

Проститься с белым светом не спешу

А я любую боль переиначу,

Я памятью обид не дорожу.

Happiness has no memory—

       you just can't find it

I checked it yesterday
And years ago.
The slightest sorrow leaves a scar behind it.
But happiness, which has no memory—

          O, no!

It's like the air—we know it's there, and

         breathe it;

It's natural, like sunshine, and like air;
And that is why

     its memory dies with it,

And we for troubles never are prepared.
When you have happiness—

      no words are needed—

It's like your heart—its place is in your breast;
Until it's pierced by pain, you never heed it,
You think you'll live

     for centuries at least.

You wonder at my smiles?

      no tears of anguish?

My lack of haste to bid this world farewell?
There is no pain on earth I cannot vanquish—
And as for insults, they can go to hell.

281

Беспамятное счастье я не выдам
Мы — вдох и выдох,
Связаны в одно.
Нас перессорить
                                бедам и обидам
Меня и счастье —
Просто не дано.

Give up my happiness which has no memory? No, never!
We're systole and diastole,
Two in one.
No insults or misfortunes
                              can dissever
My happiness and me—it simply can't be done.

Translated by Louis Zellikoff

Leonid Martynov (b. 1905) is a true virtuoso, a skilled master of language with a sensitive under-standing of the secret inner associations of words. Martynov's writing is distinguished for the peculiar harmonizing of sounds he achieves in his separate lines, verses and sometimes whole poems. At the same time Martynov is first and foremost a poet of ideas which he expresses in a vivid, original way. He belongs to this fast-moving age, responding with remarkable keenness to all that is new in this constantly changing world of ours. His intellectual curiosity is reflected in his fantastic, almost fairy-tale poems which are yet written in the spirit of scientific analysis and scientific forecasting, making a very modern impact. Leonid Martynov is one of the leading translators of Western classics and Slav poets. In 1966 he was awarded the Russian Federation State Prize.

LEONID MARTYNOV

ЛЕОНИД МАРТЫНОВ

Эхо

Что такое случилось со мною?
Говорю я с тобой одною,
А слова мои почему-то
Повторяются за стеною,
И звучат они в ту же минуту
В ближних рощах и дальних пущах,
В близлежащих людских жилищах
И на всяческих пепелищах,
И повсюду среди живущих.
Знаешь, в сущности, — это не плохо
Расстояние не помеха
Ни для смеха и ни для вздоха.
Удивительно мощное эхо!
Очевидно, такая эпоха.

Echo

It's the strangest thing!...
I speak to you, and my words ring out
All around.
They resound
In nearby streets and far-off groves,
On sites of fires and levelled graves,
In fields and woods beyond the river,
In the homes of the living....
And it's good
That it should
Be so!... Sighs, gasps, laughter
Have learnt to travel.
What's this mighty echo.
But a sign of the present epoch!

Translated by Irina Zheleznova

Что-то
Новое в мире.
Человечеству хочется песен.
Люди мыслят о лютне, о лире.
Мир без песен
Неинтересен.

Ветер,
Ветви,
Весенняя сырость,
И черны, как истлевший папирус,
Прошлогодние травы.
Человечеству хочется песен.
Люди правы.

И иду я
По этому миру.
Я хочу отыскать эту лиру,
Или — как там зовется он ныне —
Инструмент для прикосновенья
Пальцев, трепетных от вдохновенья
Города и пустыни,
Шум, подобный прибою морскому...
Песен хочется роду людскому.

Вот они, эти струны,
Будто медны и будто чугунны,
Проводов телефонных не тоньше
И не толще, должно быть.

Something new,
Something new—
Mankind thirsting for song.
Hurry up, bring lutes, bring lyres.
Of a world without song—
Yes, it's true!—
Men have tired.

Windy spring,
Running clouds,
Trees in wild flight,
Last year's grasses like time-blackened
                                    scrolls

Men are hungry for song,
Men are hungry for song,
And they're right.

Oh, to find
That proverbial lyre,
Strings like flexible wire
That respond to the fingers of genius
With a quiver ecstatic and sensuous.
Cities, deserts, the roll of the tide....
Men long, men long
For song.

Here they are, these strings—
They ring
Like bells made of copper or iron...

Умоляют:
            — О, тронь же!

Но еще не успел я потрогать —
Слышу гул отдаленный,
Будто где-то в дали туманной
За дрожащей мембраной
Выпрямляется раб обнаженный,
Исцеляется прокаженный;
Воскресает невинно казненный,
Что случилось, не может представить
— Это я! — говорит. — Это я ведь!

На деревьях рождаются листья,
Из щетины рождаются кисти,
Холст растрескивается с хрустом,
И смывается всякая плесень...
Дело пахнет искусством.
Человечеству хочется песен.

Their plea is inspired:
"Touch us, poet, come on,
We have won!"

I'm about to touch them, and suddenly hear,
Coming near
From a distance,
An insistent
And curious hum—voices, voices, voices—
Of slaves freed, no more in chains,
Of lepers cured, no more in pain,
Of the slain, the innocent slain,
Resurrected, and shouting, helpless with wonder,
"Look! It's us! We're alive again!"

New leaves on the trees are born,
New brushes are born of bristle,
Fresh sheets of canvas unroll
With an eager rustle.
Mould is washed away,
Welcome, art!
Man waits for song
With thirsting heart.

Translated by Irina Zheleznova

Вода

Вода
Благоволила
Литься!

Она
Блистала
Столь чиста,
Что — ни напиться,
Ни умыться.

И это было неспроста.

Ей
Не хватало
Ивы, тала
И горечи цветущих лоз.

Ей
Водорослей не хватало
И рыбы, жирной от стрекоз

Ей
Не хватало быть волнистой
Ей не хватало течь везде.
Ей жизни не хватало —
Чистой,
Дистиллированной
Воде!

Water

Water?
Yes, it's water.
And here we have the surety:
It follows water's laws;
It falls in drops,
It flows,
It passes all the tests of clarity and purity—
But does it serve to slake
Your thirst, or wash your clothes?

It scorns to deck its rim with rushes, reeds
                                    and sedges—
No sheen of silv'ry fish in dim mysterious deeps,
No waving water-reeds. And round its tidy edges
No song-bird sings, and ne'er a willow weeps.

Water?
Yes, it's water;
It's proved by all the data,
Although it knows no wave of storm or strife.
And this
This H_2O
This *aqua distillata*
Has all that water has—
Yes,
All but life.

Translated by Archie Johnstone

Justinas Marcinkevičius (b. 1931), a gifted Lithuanian poet of epic cast, is best known for his "Twelfth Spring", "Publicist Poem", "Blood and Ashes" (1957-1965) and has also published collections of lyric verse. He tackles a wide range of themes such as the evolution of social concepts under the influence of life's changing conditions; the individual and the community in wartime; problems of the atomic age; the individual's psychological make-up. His most popular work is the passionate anti-war poem "Blood and Ashes". Marcinkevičius has made excellent translations into Lithuanian of the Estonian epic poem "Kalevipoeg" and the Finnish "Kalevala", as well as poems by Adam Mickiewicz, Pushkin and Lermontov.

JUSTINAS MARCINKEVICIUS

ЮСТИНАС МАРЦИНКЯВИЧУС

Прелюдия

Из поэмы „КРОВЬ И ПЕПЕЛ"

Была деревня и деревни нет.
Ее сожгли живьем — со всеми.
Кто должен жить,
Кто должен умереть,
И с теми, кто на свет
Родиться должен.
Была деревня и деревни нет.

Неправда!
Есть деревня эта.
Есть!
Она горит и по сей день,
Сегодня, —
И будет до тех пор гореть, пока
Те, кто поджег деревню эту, живы.

Так расступись огонь,
Раздайся шире пламя,
Дай мне взглянуть на тех, которые горят...
Вот парень... Разве он
Мне не сказал однажды:
— Мне эта жизнь нужна затем, чтоб мог я жить

Как много он хотел и как немного!
Мой брат, ровесник мой, и почему,
О, почему ты не сказал в тот день:
— Мне эта жизнь нужна, чтобы я мог бороться.
Как горячо в моей груди!

Prelude

To the poem BLOOD AND ASHES

There was a village and it is no more.
It has been burnt alive with all its people.
With those who had to live,
With those who had to die,
And those who had as yet to come into the
                                          world.
There was a village, and it is no more.
Not true!

       The village does exist! It's there!
It's burning to this day!

            It is in flames today!
And it will go on burning while the ones
Who set it to the flames remain alive.

So part asunder, vicious blaze!
Asunder, tongues of fire!
And let me have a look at who is burning there
I know that, boy.... He was the one who told me
As I remember it, this boy had said to me:
"I need this life of mine so I can live."

How much he needed, and how little too!
My dear young friend, my brother, why did not
You say instead that fateful day:
"I need this life of mine so I can struggle!"
How hot it feels inside my breast.

Что там горит? Быть может, это сердце...
Гори, о сердце! Ты должно гореть,
Чтоб не сжигали никогда людей.

Дзукиец[1] этот, он пахал в тот день,
Пар под озимые двоил напором плуга.
Его остановили. Борозду
Не дали кончить. Плуг, вонзенный в землю
Так и остался в ней.
      Но не ржавеет он,
Нет, не ржавеет, потому что в поле
Приходит еженощно тот дзукиец
И, засучив дерюжные штаны,
Крестом он осеняется и пашет.
И протянулась эта борозда
От Пирчюписа к Панеряй,
От Панеряй к Освенциму, в Маутхаузен.
Она, как жизнь, длинна, та борозда,
И, как траншея жизни беспредельной,
Рвам смерти противостоит повсюду.

Пусть никогда не заржавеет плуг.

---

[1]— Дзукия — юго-восточная часть Литвы.

There's something burning there.
Must be my heart.
Burn bright, my heart. You've got to keep on burning
So that no people may be ever burnt alive again.

A man, a Dzukian,* was working in the field.
The fallow land he tilled for autumn sowing.
They stopped him short when he was halfway down the row
The plough he stuck into the ground where he left off
Remains there to this day.
It has not rusted.
There is no sign of rust on it because
That ploughman comes back every single night
And, rolling up his trousers made of sacking,
He says a prayer and begins to plough.
His furrow stretches on and on forever,
From Pirciupis to Panerai, from Panerai to Auschwitz,
And then again from Auschwitz to Mauthausen.
It is as infinite as life itself,
A furrow tracing life's eternal course
It challenges the trenches dug for death.

May never rust corrode that plough.

Translated by Olga Shartse

---

* Dzukia—the south-eastern part of Lithuania.

Samuel Marshak (1887-1966) was an outstanding Soviet translator and poet. As a young man, Marshak lived for a time in the house of Maxim Gorky, and the famous writer's approval of his first attempts at poetry writing played an enormous role in launching the young poet on his career. In 1911, with Gorky's assistance, Marshak went to England to continue his education and until 1914 attended lectures at London University. In 1915-16 he published his first translations of William Blake and some Scottish folk ballads. Marshak wrote lyric poems, satirical verses, plays and critical articles, but he is best known as a translator and children's writer. He translated much of Shakespeare, Shelley, Byron, Burns, Blake, Kipling, and many other poets, as well as non-Russian poets of the Soviet Union.
Marshak's poetic gift attained its peak in his "Lyric Notebook", an inspired collection on which he worked for many years. It contains philosophical reflections on life and death, meditations on the value of life and the value of art, and thoughts about time and eternity.
Samuel Marshak was awarded the Lenin Prize in 1963.

SAMUEL MARSHAK

САМУИЛ МАРШАК

Неужели я тот же самый,
Что, в постель не ложась упрямо,
Слышал первый свой громкий смех
И не знал, что я меньше всех.

И всегда-то мне дня было мало,
Даже в самые долгие дни,
Для всего, что меня занимало, —
Дружбы, драки, игры, беготни.

Да и нынче борюсь я с дремотой,
И ложусь до сих пор с неохотой,
И покою ночному не рад,
Как две трети столетья назад.

Am I dreaming, or really and truly
It was I, who in bed so unruly,
Laughed so loud for the first time one night
Not aware I was only a mite?

The days were too brief in duration,
And the longest seemed always too short—
My plans would be doomed to frustration,
Games unfinished and fights left unfought.

And I still go to bed under pressure,
In the calm of the night find no pleasure.
And in sleep I still see my worst foe
Just as three score and ten years ago.

Translated by Louis Zellikoff

Не знает вечность ни родства, ни племени
Чужда ей боль рождений и смертей.
А у меньшой сестры ее — у времени —
Бесчисленное множество детей.

Столетья разрешаются от бремени.
Плоды приносят год, и день, и час.
Пока в руках у нас частица времени,
Пускай оно работает для нас!

Пусть мерит нам стихи стопою четкою,
Работу, пляску, плаванье, полет
И — долгое оно или короткое —
Пусть вместе с нами что-то создает.

Бегущая минута незаметная
Рождает миру подвиг или стих.
Глядишь — и вечность, старая, бездетная,
Усыновит племянников своих.

Eternity knows neither kith nor kin.
The pangs of birth and death she's never known,
While Time, her younger sister, unlike her
Has countless sons and daughters of her own.

The centuries bring forth new life—and pass.
Each day, each year, each hour brings fruit untried
While we the slightest span of Time still grasp,
Let's make her serve us e'er she flies from sight.

So let our Time be filled with merry song,
With toil and dance and flights o'er space and sea;
Though brief her span, or though it last for long,
Let her, with us, create—and in creation, BE.

Unseen, into the void, the fleeting minutes soar,
Give birth to glorious deeds and poems in their race
And see—Eternity, who children never bore,
Enfolds her sister's sons in proud embrace.

Translated by Louis Zellikoff

Бессмертие

Года четыре
Был я бессмертен.
Года четыре
Был я беспечен,
Ибо не знал я о будущей смерти,
Ибо не знал я, что век мой не вечен.

Вы, что умеете жить настоящим,
В смерть, как бессмертные дети, не верьте
Миг этот будет всегда предстоящим —
Даже за час, за мгновенье до смерти.

Immortality

For four years on end
Immortal was I.
For four years on end
Light-hearted was I.
For I never knew I would die one fine day,
For I never knew I would not live for aye.

You who know how to make life sweet and pleasant,
Like children, immortal—believe not in death;
Death's time is the future—but never the present,
Though you may be breathing your very last breath.

Translated by Louis Zellikoff

Ландыш

Чернеет лес, теплом разбуженный,
Весенней сыростью объят.
А уж на ниточках жемчужины
От ветра каждого дрожат.

Бутонов круглые бубенчики
Еще закрыты и плотны,
Но солнце раскрывает венчики
У колокольчиков весны.

Природой бережно спеленутый,
Завернутый в зеленый лист,
Растет цветок в глуши нетронутой
Прохладен, хрупок и душист.

Томится лес весною раннею,
И всю счастливую тоску
И все свое благоухание
Он отдал горькому цветку.

Lily of the Valley

Stirred by the first faint ice-free pulse,
The forest, grumbling, clings to winter's sleep
But spring's own pearls, strung onto threads of green
Quiver with life at every breath of wind.

Like tender human babe in swaddling clothes
The newborn nestled in her funneled leaf,
And now within her maiden bower she grows
Fragrant, vulnerable, exquisite.

Fragile flower and thick limbed forest share
The bitter sweetness of the fevered spring,
The agony of life's slow-thawing veins
The ecstasy of life's thrusting growth.

Translated by Archie Johnstone

На всех часах вы можете прочесть
Слова простые истины глубокой:
Теряя время, мы теряем честь.
А совесть остается после срока.

Она живет в душе не по часам.
Раскаянье всегда приходит поздно.
А честь на час указывает нам
Протянутой рукою — стрелкой грозной.

Чтоб наша совесть не казнила нас,
Не потеряйте краткий этот час.
Пускай, как стрелки в полдень, будут вместе
Веленья нашей совести и чести!

On every clock this message you can find—
Its simple words a truth profound contains—
Who squanders time, casts honour to the wind,
Though Time expires, your conscience will remain.

It dwells within the soul, not heeding hours;
Repentance always comes a bit too late,
While honour points towards the fleeting hours
With outstretched finger, like the hand of fate.

To keep your conscience from reproaches free,
Lose not one hour, however brief it be;
Just as at noon the clock's two hands together
                                        stand,
Let honour always go with conscience hand-in-hand.

Translated by Louis Zellikoff

Eduardas Mieželaitis (b. 1919) is a popular Lithuanian poet and 1962 Lenin Prize winner. "All that I have written is really a lyrical monologue on the time-honoured theme of Man and his stubborn battle against humiliation, oppression and need," he wrote. "Man is the most precious thing on Earth. Man is my first, my truest love and my constant concern." Mieželaitis is the author of about twenty books (the first one was published in 1943) but he is best known for his book of philosophical lyric poetry entitled "Man", about which he wrote: "I travelled along many long roads before I arrived at the thoughts and conclusions which I have set out in this book." The style of his intellectual and emotional verse is free, and the images are hyperbolic. Many of the verses are hymns to the powerful intellect of Man, the toiler and fighter who has harnessed atomic energy and explored outer space. The poem "Man" has had a great influence on the shaping of many of our young poets.

EDUARDAS MIEŽELAITIS

ЭДУАРДАС МЕЖЕЛАЙТИС

Пепел

Эта рыжая пыль под ногами, щебенка
Из костей, — не осколки ль, покрытые ржой?
Это, может быть, резвые ножки ребенка,
Что за белою бабочкой гнался межой;
Или ручки, — дитя ими тянется к маме,
Обнимая за шею, ласкается к ней...
Или был этот щебень большими руками,
Что с любовью к груди прижимали детей.
Этот пепел, который разносится с ветром,
Был глазами, смеялся и плакал порой,
Был губами, улыбкою, музыкой,

светом,

Поцелуями был этот пепел седой.
Был сердцами, тревогою, радостью, мукой;
Был мозгами, сплетеньем извилин

живых, —

Слово «жить» до конца, словно буква за

буквой

Точно белым по черному вписано в них.
Эти волосы — локоны, косы и пряди,
Что навалены мертвой косматой горой,
Кто-нибудь расплетал и взволнованно гладил,
И сухими губами касался порой.
Чистый трепет сердец, вдохновенные речи,
Золотые надежды, сияние глаз...
Крематориев страшных горящие печи.
Пепел... Пепел... Лишь пепел остался

от вас.

Ashes

These russet-hued ashes, the gravel of bones underneath
Like the rust-covered splinters of less than two decades
ago—
What were they—a shepherd-boy's bare, sunburnt feet
Running after a butterfly as it would flit to and fro?
Or the tiny, soft elbows and hands of a child
Round the neck of a mother whose ashes lie here with the
rest?
Or the arms of a man, big and strong, yet so mild
As they fondled a baby pressed close to his breast?
Aye, these rust-coloured ashes the wind now strews over
the fields
Shone in eyes that had clouded with tears, gleamed and
laughed with delight,
Glowed as hearts that had felt all a living heart feels,
Smiled as lips that were somebody's music and light,
Burned with passion, knew pleasure, anxiety, pain,
Could forget and remember, accuse and reproach and
forgive,
Throbbed with thought in the intricate cells of a brain,
Nurtured dreams and desires, wished to love and be loved,
yearned to live!
And this hair—all these locks, all these plaits, all
these curls
Lying heaped in a lifeless and orderless pile,
That hot fingers would twine and untwine to the murmur
of passionate words,
That hot lips would touch softly and linger a while.
Hopes of happiness, dreams of pure joy that can now
never be,
The glitter of eyes—huge, reflecting the light of the
soul—
Burned in dread crematorium fires by inhuman decree,
Ashes, only these ashes are left of them all.

Пролетая над проволокой колючей,
Птица мягко касается краем крыла
Дикой розы, на диво багровой и жгучей,
Что на этой кровавой земле расцвела.
Боль, которой еще мое сердце не знало,
Превратилась в колючий, соленый комок
И, как пуля, в гортани навеки застряла,
Чтоб дышать я не мог и забыть я не мог
Я тяжелый, невидящий взгляд

подними́маю

И от неба его не могу отвести,
Всем своим существом к человеку

взываю,

Человеческий пепел сжимая в горсти.

Освенцим.

Flying over the remnants of barbed wire, a bird from
the forest
Unexplainably hesitant, hovers around and around
A wild rose, of all roses the reddest and saddest
That had chosen to bloom on this blood-sodden ground.
And a pain—how, I wonder, my heart can endure it—
Of a sharpness never experienced yet
Tears and pierces my flesh like a bullet
Bedded deep in my throat, not to let me draw breath or
forget.
Overwhelmed by the horrors, unhearing, unseeing,
Unable to stir with the weight of the anguish I feel,
With the dust of the dead in my hand, from the depths
of my being
To all who are living today I appeal!

Translated by Dorian Rottenberg

Губы

Губы — красною лентой,
Словно флаг, что разодран в бою.
— Это есть наш последний! —
Я с друзьями пою.
Эти губы не в силах
Жить без сладости ягод,

                      и соли морской

И небес темно-синих,
И беседы мужской.
Губы ждут папирос,
Губы жаждут и меда, и чаю.
И на каждый проклятый вопрос
Я немедленно отвечаю.
Приоткрытые губы
Подобны гнезду.

            И душа

В этой теми и глуби
Выводит слова не спеша.

Если губы устали,
Если сжаты они — разожми,
Чтобы птичьею стаей
Летели слова над людьми.
Чтобы каждое слово,
Словно птица, летало везде.
И душа чтобы снова
Выводила их в том же гнезде.

Lips

Lips like scarlet ribbons parting,
Or a banner that fierce fighting rends—
"...'tis the final conflict starting..."
I am singing with friends.
For those lips not to perish
They need sweetness of berries,
                            the sea's briny smell
They need blue skies we cherish.
Conversation as well.
Lips may hold cigarettes,
Lips for tea and for honey are yearning.
Every question men ask me is met
By an answer from my lips returning.
Those two lips when half open
Are dark as a nest
                        where the heart,
Hatching thoughts to be spoken,
Unhurriedly lets them depart.

When your tense lips are feeling
Tired and weak, make them open again.
Like a flock of birds wheeling
Send your words winging high for all men.
When your lips have once freed them,
Let those words sweep the skies like the birds.
Your soul had to breed them,
But now in its nest again let it brood over words.

319

Временами с трибуны
С губ срываются, словно из туч,
Громы, молнии, бури,
Но гроза миновала,

          и светится солнечный луч
Губы — радужной аркой
На безоблачном небе лица,
И — счастливый и жаркий
Поцелуй без конца!
Слышит женщина, слышит
То, что мы говорить ей должны,
Хоть слова эти тише
Самой тихой земной тишины.
Словно маки, сливаются,
И огнем занимается мак,
Губы в губы вливаются
Сочно-красные

          в темных домах.
Утром — ясным и добрым —
Слышишь песню проснувшихся птиц.
Вместе с птицами —
Веселый и бодрый —

          песню свистишь.
И походкою ветра,
Словно ветер

         меж прочих ветров,
Повторяешь за ветром
Его песню без слов.
Тихо. Тихо.
Алыми и прохладными,
К небу — жадными,
К радости — жадными
Губами.

Lips a tribune's call sounding
Can hurl words like a bolt from the clouds,
Setting thunder resounding.
But the danger once past
                    we see sunbeams can pierce
                              sombre shrouds.

Lips may be rainbow arcs bending
Through the sky of an untroubled face—
Clinging kiss without ending,
Joyful, ardent embrace.
Women hear words yet unspoken—
Words we owe them extolling their worth—
In the silence unbroken,
As profound as our earth.
Like poppies, lips fusing
Fill with passion, till flowers ignite,
Their warm essence diffusing,
Richly red
         in the shadows of night.
When a new day is dawning
And the birds make the lucent air ring
You will whistle
To welcome the morning
                    and with the birds sing.
Fresh and bright as the wind,
You repeat
         the wind's song you have heard,
Soft and light as the wind,
With a lilt, but no word.
Softly, so softly,
Songs linger on cool scarlet lips
That for heaven are longing,
For joys ever longing—
                    Those lips....

Translated by Tom Botting

321

Alexander Mezhirov (b. 1923) began writing poetry during the war. His first efforts were clearly inspired by Blok, but then the harsh realities of war imposed their own, stronger influence on his poetry. His work bears the imprint—more distinctly than does that of his contemporaries—of the tragedy of those who grew up in war. It speaks of the sobering pain of broken illusions, of learning humaneness by mastering one's egotism and of the search for a source of spiritual support in those years of fire, bloodshed and death. Mezhirov was wounded and demobbed, and in 1943 he entered the Gorky Literary Institute in Moscow. His first collection of poetry entitled "It's a Long Road" came out in 1947. His best known books are "Poems" (1957), "Windshield" (1961) and "Farewell to Snow" (1964).

ALEXANDER MEZHIROV

АЛЕКСАНДР МЕЖИРОВ

Музыка

АЛЕКСАНДР МЕЖИРОВ

АЛЕКСАНДР МЕЖИРОВ

Какая музыка была!
Какая музыка играла,
Когда и души и тела
Война проклятая попрала.

Какая музыка
                    во всем,
Всем и для всех —
                              не по ранжиру
Осилим... Выстоим... Спасем...
Ах, не до жиру, — быть бы живу

Солдатам головы кружа,
Трехрядка
                    под накатом бревен
Была нужней для блиндажа,
Чем для Германии Бетховен.

И через всю страну
                              струна
Натянутая трепетала,
Когда проклятая война
И души и тела топтала.

Стенали яростно,
                              навзрыд
Одной-единой страсти ради
На полустанке — инвалид
И Шостакович — в Ленинграде.

Sprites of Music

When war, the cursed, bloody war
Our souls and bodies smote and shattered,
The sprites of music wept and swore,
They wailed and sang and roared and stuttered

Theirs was a mighty overture
Addressed to all
                without distinction:
We'll fight....
          We'll win....
                     We will endure,
Surviving bloodshed and destruction!

In dugouts songs rang out galore,
Accordions bayed as loud as demons,
And to the men these tunes meant more
Than did Beethoven to the Germans.

Across the land,
              from shore to shore,
A string stretched taut, unceasing, quivered
When war, the cursed, bloody war
Our souls and bodies crushed and shivered.

A crippled soldier in a square
And Shostakovich on the Neva
In raging sound
            their hearts laid bare,
By one resolve and passion driven.

Translated by Irina Zheleznova

Февраль

Шаг один от февраля до марта

НИКОЛАЙ ТАРАСОВ

I

Вот из ворот арбатского двора
Она выходит, равнодушно глядя.
В нещипаном бобре солидный дядя
На тротуаре топчется.
Пора!

Пора, пора вершить еще одно,
Еще одно последнее свиданье,
То, о котором решено заране,
Что ничего не выйдет все равно.

В проулок приарбатский из ворот
Она выходит, скроенная ладно,
И повернуть ей хочется обратно,
Но не обратно, а туда идет.

Две девочки застыли на бегу,
Во все глаза следят завороженно
За шубкой из пушистого нейлона,
За тонкой бровью, выгнутой в дугу.

В младенческом неведенье своем
Они запоминают все детали:
Ах, как воздушен газ ее вуали!
Как у нее высок ноги подъем!

February

One step from February to March

NIKOLAI TARASOV

I

She passes through the gateway, tall and slim,
Her face with its unchanging wintry pallor
Impassive....

A stout man in beaver collar
Stamps up and down the pavement...
It is time!

It's time, it's time for one last tryst, one more
Delicious, brief, but oh, such painful meeting,
Of which she knows and cannot help repeating
That it will come to nothing as before

She pauses for a moment in the street,
Her graceful figure tense with hesitation....
Will she go back?...

With fresh determination
She walks ahead, reluctant to retreat.

Two little girls stop short as she goes by,
And watch her every movement, fascinated....
Her ease, her polish, the exaggerated
Arch of her brow above the deep-set eye.

They note in open, innocent delight
All of the special little things about her,
Admire her shoes, her gauzy scarf, and whisper:
"That coat's a dream! So fluffy and so light."

327

Ну что глядите, — думает она. —
Не дай вам бог... А, впрочем, ведь когда-то
И ты пленялась дивами Арбата...
Да что там ты! Не только ты одна.

Но твой беспечный разум не постиг,
Что все, что старо, и что все, что юно,
Мечтало и мечтает обоюдно
Местами поменяться хоть на миг.

И вот машина в ночь тебя увозит
От девочек, от дома, от ворот.
Еще февраль бодрится и морозит,
Но и мороз-то сам уже не тот.

2

Летит сосулька из зимы в весну
И, перед тем как сделаться водою,
Звенит, исходит песней молодою
И гонит сон и клонит не ко сну.

Проулок ваш не узок, не широк,
И окна в окна смотрят не мигая,
И, по карнизу шибко пробегая,
Тревожит занавеску ветерок.

Ваш двор как перевернутый колодезь,
На дне колодца — небо, как вода.
В ту воду вы однажды окунетесь
И захлебнетесь ею навсегда.

Что там творится в мире заоконном?!
Зима в исходе, видно по всему.
Давайте вместе слушать, как со звоном
Летит сосулька из зимы в весну.

"Why must they stare?" she asks herself, and sighs
"God help them." Then, her mood now wistful, mellow.
"I too once loved Arbat* and used to follow
Its marvels, awed, with watchful, jealous eyes."

And this indeed was true, she had.... And yet
The fact that youth and age with one another
Of changing places dream, she did not bother
To think about, and so could not admit.

Far from the gate, the girls, the gaping street,
She drives away into the whirling darkness.
The February frost has lost its sharpness
And almost seems aware of its defeat.

2

An icicle from winter into spring
Drops tunefully and, jangling, falls to pieces,
And as it slowly melts it never ceases,
Defying sleep, its gleeful song to sing.

Your street is not too narrow, nor too wide;
The windows meet each other's gaze, unblinking.
A playful wind, across the ledges sprinting,
Plucks at the curtains and will not subside.

Your courtyard is a well turned upside down,
The blue of sky is like the purest water....
You'll dip in it one fateful day when winter
Gives way to spring,
                    and, drunk with rapture, drown.

The world outside, still cold and shivering,
Is clad in snowy robes that gleam and glisten.
An icicle—come, hold your breath and listen—
Drops tunefully from winter into spring.

Translated by Irina Zheleznova

* Arbat—busy street in the centre of Moscow

Sergei Mikhalkov (b. 1913) is a widely known children's poet and satirical writer. There can hardly be a child in the Soviet Union who does not know his poetry by heart. Mikhalkov has written humorous verses, songs, fables, feuilletons, plays ("Conceited Rabbit" and "Sombrero") and screenplays ("The New Adventures of Puss in Boots" and others). He is also chief editor of "Fitil" (Fuse), a weekly series of short satirical films which was started several years ago. Mikhalkov has translated "Three Little Pigs" into Russian and many other nursery rhymes and stories for children.

SERGEI MIKHALKOV

СЕРГЕЙ МИХАЛКОВ

Сатирик и сапер

Сатирик похож на сапера, друзья, —
Минирует он, и минирую я!
Задача сапера, коль в корень смотреть,
Врага подорвать, самому уцелеть.
Но если ты дрожь ощущаешь в руках,
Бросай свою службу в саперных войсках
Ведь есть же на свете другие посты —
Ну, скажем, писать наградные листы!
Здесь следует тоже сноровку иметь,
Чтоб лист без помарки оформить суметь

The Satyrist and the Sapper

The satyrist acts like the sapper, you know:
They both lay their mines to get rid of the foe.
Yes, to blow up the foe and themselves to stay whole
Is the sapper's and satyrist's ultimate goal.

But if you feel shaky at mention of war
Then better not enter the Sappers' Corps.
There's plenty of posts where you don't have to kill,
For instance, the one where award lists you fill.
There's a snag here, too, namely: the skill that it
takes
To fill in a blank-form without mistakes.

Translated by Dorian Rottenberg

Журавль и Хавронья

В «Лесных Пенатах»,
На выставке картин художников пернатых,
Произошел неслыханный скандал:
Портретом журавля Хавронья возмутилась,
Как на базаре с ним при всех сцепилась,
И тот в сердцах ей по загривку дал!
Все началось, как я сказал, с портрета.
Хавронья хрюкнула: «Как выставляют это?»
«Что именно?» — послышалось в ответ.
«Да всю эту мазню, включая ваш портрет!»
«Позвольте!..»
«Да! Да! Да! Вы не туда идете!» —
«Помилуйте»!
   «Погрязли вы в болоте!»
«Да как вы смеете?!»
     «Как смела до сих пор!..»
Печально кончился
   «дискуссионный» спор...
Но что по существу Хавронью так задело!
Хотите знать?
   Тут вот в чем было дело:
Журавль был графиком — он клювом рисовал,
Хавронья пятачком картины малевала.
Мазков на полотне Журавль не признавал,
Штрихов на полотне Свинья не признавала.

The Crane and the Pig

At Woodland Gallery, a year or two ago,
When works by feathered artists were on show
There suddenly broke out a dreadful scandal.
Employing language fit but for a vandal,
"I say,"
Quoth Mrs. Pig, "who put this on display?"
"What do you mean?" the Crane retorted.
"Why, all this mess, including your own portrait."
"Excuse me,..."
        "Yes, oh yes! Is that the way to paint?"
"I beg your pardon, but..."
           "Most certainly it ain't!"
"Now, don't you think you've gone too far, my friend?"
Need I recount the whole discussion to the end?
What was it, though, made Mrs. Pig so sore?
You want to know?
        Well, here's the matter's core:

Engraver Crane, who used his beak to etch
Thought painting worthy only of a wretch.
For paintress Pig, who daubed her colours with her
                       snout,
Engraving wasn't art—beyond all doubt!

Translated by Dorian Rottenberg

О дураке

С хвоста — коня бояться надо,
С рогов — корову и быка,
Со всех сторон, с любого взгляда
Бояться надо дурака!

Когда дурак сидит на месте,
Где умный должен был сидеть,
Там нам его, сказать по чести,
Подчас пе просто разглядеть.

Дурак и вежливым бывает,
И не всегда на всех рычит.
Красноречиво выступает,
Многозначительно молчит.

Дурак один такое может
Наворотить и там и тут,
Что сотня умных не поможет.
Сто мудрецов не разберут.

Но, как в народе говорится,
Управа есть и на него:
Насмешки даже тот боится,
Кто не боится ничего!

The Fool

A horse should be feared from the tail-end, my friend
From the fore-end—the cow and the bull.
But—
    from all points of view,
                       from beginning to end,
Beware, beware of the fool!

Whenever a fool is installed in the place
Intended by right for the wise
The fool's true identity promptly to trace
Is hard for the keenest of eyes.

For sometimes a fool may be glib and polite,
Not at all an inveterate brute.
The fool may be able to speak and to write
Or to be quite impressively mute.

One fool single-handed can muddle, my friend,
So much in a moment's course
That ten hundred men will be helpless to mend
By wisdom, patience or force.

But here we may mention a general rule
To be followed by wise men hereafter:
Though there's plentiful reasons to fear a fool,
Remember: a fool fears laughter!

Translated by Dorian Rottenberg

Sergei Narovchatov (b. 1919) interrupted his education in 1939 to volunteer for the Finnish front, enrolled at the Literary Institute when he came back and then joined up again when Hitler invaded Russia. He began by writing poetry about the war and still frequently returns to war themes.

The mood of his poetry is highly romantic, and his handling of lofty subjects is remarkably subtle and stirringly profound, without a trace of affectation.

Narovchatov is an essentially Russian poet. He turns again and again to Russia's heroic history, her wide open spaces, her people, her legends and her songs, which provide the substance of such poems as "Vasily Buslayev", "The Song About Ataman Semyon Dezhnev". His admiration for Lermontov must have inspired him to write the book "Lermontov's Lyricism", a serious and competent study. Narovchatov's reviews and articles on modern poetry often appear in the Soviet press.

SERGEI NAROVCHATOV

СЕРГЕЙ НАРОВЧАТОВ

В те годы

Я проходил, скрипя зубами, мимо
Сожженных сел, казненных городов
По горестной, по русской, по родимой,
Завещанной от дедов и отцов.

Запоминал над деревнями пламя.
И ветер, разносивший жаркий прах,
И девушек, библейскими гвоздями
Распятых па райкомовских дверях.

И воронье кружилось без боязни,
И коршун рвал добычу на глазах,
И метил все бесчинства и все казни
Паучий извивающийся знак.

В своей печали древним песням равный
Я села, словно летопись, листал
И в каждой бабе видел Ярославну,
Во всех ручьях Непрядву узнавал.

Крови своей, своим святыням верный,
Слова старинные я повторял скорбя:
— Россия, мати! Свете мой безмерный
Которой местью мстить мне за тебя!

Those Years

Grating my teeth in pain, I passed
Burned-down village and tortured town;
Through war-torn Russia, my very own,
The heritage of a cherished past.

They sank in my heart, the tossing flames,
The smouldering windswept ashes,
Girls crucified in the streets and lanes,
On doors and window sashes.

The ravens gorged without shame or fear,
The buzzards clawed corpses bare and stark,
And all the horrors both far and near
Were marked with the crawling spider's mark.

Watching the widows bent with their woes
I re-felt the sorrow of ancient songs,
At one with the trees in their mournful rows,
With the streams running tears at the country's
                                                    wrongs.

I passed by ruins to find still more,
Through my country scathed by the flames of war.
"Russia, mother, light of my eyes,
Can any revenge suffice?"

                              Translated by Dorian Rottenberg

За советскую власть!

Давних годов пионерские сборы!
Мальчишкам в огне языкатых костров
Чудилось пламя орудий «Авроры»
И высверк буденновских быстрых клинков.

Кому из вихрастых тогда не мечталось
В геройском бою по-геройскому пасть,
Чтоб только три слова на камне осталось:
  За советскую власть!

Мальчишки мужали, мальчишки взрослели,
И только бы жить начинать сорванцам,
Как их завертели такие метели,
Какие, пожалуй, не снились отцам.

И кто в сорок первом, а кто в сорок пятом
Всю душу вложив в неделимую страсть,
Сложил свою голову честным солдатом
  За советскую власть!

Я помню вас в горьких и праведных буднях
Без вас мы кончали победой войну,
Без вас запускали мы на небо спутник,
Без вас поднимали в степях целину.

Но со всем поколением в сердце несу я
Вашего сердца нетленную часть.
Навек присягаю, навек голосую
  За советскую власть!

For Soviet Power!

Meetings of Young Pioneers... oh, how distant!
Aurora's* guns blaze in the fire-lit glade—
Boys seeing visions in bonfire tongues leaping,
They see the quick flash of Budyonny's blade.

Which of these tousled ones, then, was not dreaming
Of dying a hero in some battled hour?
And leaving three words on a stone as a reminder:
                                    For Soviet Power!

Young boys taking manhood, young boys waking adult,
So wild and untried on the threshold of life;
But still they endured the war blizzard so blinding:
Fierce, beyond dreams of their fathers, that strife.

Each put his whole soul into one single passion,
Those years, forty-one, forty-five; when the flower
Of youth—honest soldiers—was spent for the nation,
                                    For Soviet Power!

'Tis you I remember, on good days and bad days,
You absent—in victory, when War Two was won;
You absent—when Sputnik was launched to the
                                    space-ways,
When virgin, brown steppes were exposed to the sun.

Today's living, and I, in our heart of hearts carry
A part of your hearts, like an undying flower.
And I stake my oath, cast my vote, and forever,
                                    For Soviet Power!

Translated by Gladys Evans

* Cruiser *Aurora* fired the first shot to signal the
start of the October Revolution, 1917.

Boris Pasternak (1890-1960) was a poet of world stature whose genius was complex and contradictory. The son of a well-known painter, he was taught composition by Scriabin and received his philosophical education in Germany; thus Pasternak absorbed the quintessence of twentieth century culture. His withdrawal from the trivia of life and the bustle of the surrounding world was an intrinsic part of his nature. At the same time he lived an inner life that was packed to ten times the normal capacity, and in his poetry responded sensitively to all the major, cardinal changes in the world. His early poetry was perhaps overcomplicated in form, but his later style was classically clear. By constructing his poetry on several planes at once, by using his own original syntax and the associative linking of images, he revealed the essence of phenomena and brought out their philosophical content with superb skill.

Boris Pasternak was also an outstanding Russian translator of Shakespeare and Goethe.

BORIS PASTERNAK

БОРИС ПАСТЕРНАК

Быть знаменитым некрасиво.
Не это подымает ввысь.
Не надо заводить архива,
Над рукописями трястись.

Цель творчества — самоотдача,
А не шумиха, не успех.
Позорно, ничего не знача,
Быть притчей на устах у всех.

Но надо жить без самозванства,
Так жить, чтобы в конце концов
Привлечь к себе любовь пространства
Услышать будущего зов.

И надо оставлять пробелы
В судьбе, а не среди бумаг,
Места и главы жизни целой
Отчеркивая на полях.

И окунаться в неизвестность,
И прятать в ней свои шаги,
Как прячется в тумане местность,
Когда в чей не видать ни зги.

Другие по живому следу
Пройдут твой путь за пядью пядь,

It's unbecoming to be famous.
It isn't that that lifts aloft.
Maintaining archives tends to maim us.
Hoard MSS and you are lost.

The aim of art is self-discharge
And not the clap-trap of success.
It's shameless to be looming large
For merits which are but a guess.

Live on through life without imposture,
Live so as in the final end
To hear the love-call of the future,
Expanse and distance to befriend.

Hiatus—leave them in your fortune
But not by any means in papers.
Although the process be a torture,
Let whole chapters of life escape us.

And ducking down into obscurity,
Conceal your steps beneath its cloak.
So landscapes sometimes hide their purity
Beneath a veil of fog or smoke.

Though others will retrace in hot
Pursuit the imprints of your feet,

Но пораженья от победы
Ты сам не должен отличать.

И должен ни единой долькой
Не отступаться от лица,
Но быть живым, живым и только
Живым и только до конца.

Remember: you yourself must not
Distinguish triumph from defeat.

Not even by the slightest fraction
Must you your proper self transcend.
Just be alive, in thought and action,
Alive and always to the end.

Translated by Dorian Rottenberg

Ева

Стоят деревья у воды,
И полдень с берега крутого
Закинул облака в пруды,
Как переметы рыболова.

Как невод, тонет небосвод,
И в это небо, точно в сети,
Толпа купальщиков плывет —
Мужчины, женщины и дети.

Пять-шесть купальщиц в лозняке
Выходят на берег без шума
И выжимают на песке
Свои купальные костюмы.

И наподобие ужей
Ползут и вьются кольца пряжи,
Как будто искуситель-змей
Скрывался в мокром трикотаже.

О женщина, твой вид и взгляд
Ничуть меня в тупик не ставят.
Ты вся — как горла перехват,
Когда его волненье сдавит.

Ты создана как бы вчерне,
Как строчка из другого цикла,

Eve

On shore the trees stand looking on
While midday casts the clouds on bet
Into the meditative pond
For want of any other net.

And like a net the sky sinks in
The pensively expectant waters
And into it the bathers swim,
Fathers, mothers, sons and daughters.

Then half a dozen girls come out
Without a stir among the shoots
And rivulets of water spout
As they wring out their bathing suits

And, firing the imagination,
The coils of fabric coil and twist
As though the serpent of temptation
Had really marked them for its nest.

O woman, on vour looks I dote,
But have no mental blanks to fill;
You're like the stricture in a throat
Seized by an unexpected thrill.

You seem created as a draft,
A stanza from another sequence,

Как будто не шутя во сне
Из моего ребра возникла.

И тотчас вырвалась из рук
И выскользнула из объятья
Сама — смятенье и испуг
И сердца мужеского сжатье.

As if indeed the handicraft
Of somebody who knew no equals,

Made of my rib while asleep I lay,
You broke the clasping arms apart,
The very image of dismay,
A spasm that grips and wrings man's heart.

Translated by Dorian Rottenberg

Когда разгуляется

Большое озеро как блюдо.
За ним — скопленье облаков,
Нагроможденных белой грудой
Суровых горных ледников.

По мере смены освещенья
И лес меняет колорит:
То весь горит, то черной тенью
Насевшей копоти покрыт.

Когда в исходе дней дождливых
Меж туч проглянет синева,
Как небо празднично в прорывах
Как торжества полна трава!

Стихает ветер, даль расчистив.
Разлито солнце по земле.
Просвечивает зелень листьев,
Как живопись в цветном стекле.

В церковной росписи оконниц
Так в вечность смотрят изнутри
В мерцающих венцах бессонниц
Святые, схимники, цари.

Как будто внутренность собора
Простор земли, и чрез окно

When the Weather Clears

A dish-like lake, serene and spacious,
Converging stormclouds overhead
And there, beyond, the alpine glaciers,
Lustrous and stark, sublime and dread.

The lighting alters and the woods
Go through a constant change of colour,
Now burning, now beneath a hood
Of heart-oppressing, ash-like dolour.

When at the end of rainy days
The heavy clouds abruptly pass
What festive blue the sky displays
And how triumphant looks the grass.

The wind dies down, the distance clears,
Bright sunshine floods the hills and plains
And then the foliage appears
Like paintings seen through stained-glass pane

So from illumined chapel-windows
Saints, hermits, tsars and bishopry
Each in his brightly shining nimbus
Look out upon eternity.

I too am sometimes blessed to hear them,
The distant echoes of the choir,

Далекий отголосок хора
Мне слышать иногда дано.

Природа, мир, тайник вселенной
Я службу долгую твою,
Объятый дрожью сокровенной,
В слезах от счастья отстою.

As if inside a vast cathedral—
The earth's expanse in grand attire.

My world, my universe, my nature,
Your livelong service to the end
With a believer's palpitation,
With tears of gladness I'll attend.

Translated by Dorian Rottenberg

Alexander Prokofiev (b 1900) is a well-known bard of the Russian north. He was born and raised in the family of a fisherman His early poetry (the first book "Midday" came out in 1931) is distinguished for its emotional spontaneity, colourful idiom and revolutionary enthusiasm. During the Great Patriotic War he wrote a poem called "Russia" which became an immensely popular lyric song. Prokofiev, who paints wonderful word-pictures of the Russian landscape, makes extensive use of traditional Russian poetic means, rhythms, idioms, and folk-song metaphors. His reflections on life, which make up the content of his most recent poetry, are set in the form of lyrical parables.

In 1961, Alexander Prokofiev was awarded the Lenin Prize.

ALEXANDER PROKOFIEV

АЛЕКСАНДР ПРОКОФЬЕВ

Из биографии

Я хожу не по графику
По тропинкам и мхам.
Вся моя биография
Разошлась по стихам.

Вся — от красного флага
До ломтя на столе,
Вся — от первого шага
По родимой земле.

Вся — от песни певучей,
Что зовем и поем,
До былины дремучей
В Заонежье моем.

От подснежников милых
На вешней заре
До отцовской могилы
На старом бугре.

Вся — от листьев опалых
До весенних ветвей,
До звезды пятипалой
На папахе моей.

Мы, где надо, не трафили
Ни чужим, ни родне...
Вся моя биография
На родной стороне:

My Biography

My agenda's no mystery—
Life's steep byroads I climb,
And the whole of my history
Is depicted in rhyme.

All—from red banner soaring
To the bread in my hand,
From first footsteps, exploring,
That I made o'er my land,

From old memories clinging,
That with present entwine,
To the folksongs they're singing
In that homeland of mine,

From the snowdrops that hurried
Through the winter's last snow
To the grave where they buried
My old folks long ago.

All—from dry leaves descending
To the spring's stirring sap,
To the five rays extending
From the star on my cap.

I have made no concessions,
Not to stranger nor wife....
My land has my confessions,
Has the tale of my life.

Не в какой-то ограде,
А в ветрах верховых,
И в походной тетради,
И в стихах фронтовых,

И в делах, и в опале,
Той, что лютой зовут,
И в друзьях, что отпали,
И в друзьях, что живут.

Кто-то вечно под тучами,
День за днем — ни строки
Где-то слово замучили,
Зажимая в тиски.

Ну их к дьяволу с квотой
Утверждающей лень,
И глубинной зевотой,
Низвергающей день!

Я же знаю дорогу,
Путь извечный, крутой,
И пока, слава богу,
Не знаком с немотой!

Not in lone shelter hiding,
But in wind's frenzied roar,
In notes jotted while striding,
And in poems of war,

In disfavour that smarted,
And in deeds that have shone,
In the friends now departed,
And in those that live on.

Some are never contented—
Not a line all the day—
All the words they've tormented,
But have nothing to say.

May their quotas go perish,
That just help them to laze,
And the languor they cherish,
That just wastes all their days.

But I know where I'm going,
That the way's hard and long,
And, thank God, I'm o'erflowing
For the present with song.

Translated by Eugene Felgenhauer

Возвращение

Не орел такие вести и не ветер нам принес —
Возвратились наши парни, что летали возле
                                              звезд.

Вот веселье так веселье в нашем песенном
                                              краю,
Я других забот не знаю, я о нем сейчас пою.

Говорить бы с ним гудками океанских кораблей
Одарить его б венками с наших благостных
                                              полей,

Громкой песней соловьиной там, где реки и гаи
Только жаль, что в эту пору отгремели соловьи.

Но простор цветной разбужен
И небес подъята высь,
Мы веселью честно служим,
Спозаранку поднялись!

Мы взвиваем что попало —
Полушалки и платки,
От велика и до мала
Стали на ногу легки.

Вот какое видя дело,
Золотых парней хваля,
Заплясала, зазвенела
Наша русская земля.

Their Return

Not the eagle, nor the wild wind have such tidings
                              brought to me,
But our lads who'd been a-sailing through the endless,
                                        starry sea.
Joy and gladness, joy and gladness over all our country
                                              ring,
I've no worries in the world. tis of merriment I sing.
How I wish I could announce it with the hoots of ships
                                        at sea,
How I wish I could bedeck it with some flowers
                              from the lea,
With the nightingale's sweet ballads that o'er stream
                                    and forest ring,
Only trouble is the songbirds in this season do not sing!

> But the space above's been shaken,
> Heaven's dome much higher raised;
> Merriment we've not forsaken—
> Since the dawn we haven't lazed.
>
> Everyone in welcome waving
> Caps and kerchiefs in the street;
> Even old, like young behaving,
> Have grown lighter on their feet.
>
> Seeing such a welcome ringing
> For our lads on every hand,
> Gaily dancing, loudly singing
> Is our native Russian land.

Вся — с полями и лесами
С хороводами красавиц —
И звенит, и звенит,
Чем наш край знаменит:

Песней,
Удалью,
Молодечеством...

Ой, Россия,
Русь.
Мое Отечество!

Every field and copse rejoices,
With the singing maiden voices,
Is repeating o'er and o'er
What our land is famous for:

For its
Rousing songs,
For its fearlessness...

Russia,
Land of mine,
Land of peerlessness!

Translated by Eugene Felgenhauer

Хлеб

На столе простом
Хлеб
С капустным листом,
С угольком на исподе.
Мы с него глаз не сводим
Десять душ,
Десять душ.
Мама, рушь,
Мама, рушь,
Мама, режь
Поскорей
На сынов и дочерей.
Режь, режь много раз!
Это просьба наших глаз!
Дай мне с угольком,
С тем погасшим огоньком!
Мама, рушь,
Мама, режь!
Мамушка,
Сама поешь!..

Bread

The table is spread
With nothing
But bread,
Home-made and browned.
We all sit spell-bound.
Ten souls today,
Ten souls today,
Mother, cut away,
Mother, cut away,
That your sons and daughters
The quicker may
Eat a piece of bread
Cut without delay!
That is what our eyes all say!
Let me have the brownest part,
With the fire still breathing in its heart!
Cut, cut,
Mother, do!
Mother,
Eat a little too!

Translated by Eugene Felgenhauer

Robert Rozhdestvensky (b 1932) is one of our most popular young poets, and a follower of Mayakovsky whose belief that modern poetry should be based on real fact he shares. His style is dramatic and direct. Using Robert Rozhdestvensky's poems, the composer Dmitri Kabalevsky has written a "Requiem", in memory of those who died in the war against fascism. "Letters to the Thirtieth Century" and "Sputnik Calling" are the most interesting of Robert Rozhdestvensky's collections of poetry.

ROBERT ROZHDESTVENSKY

РОБЕРТ РОЖДЕСТВЕНСКИЙ

Половина

ВОИНАМ ПОДВИГА ГЛАВОЙ

РОВЕН РОЖДЕН ГЕРОИЧЕСКИЙ

Хитрозадые цари,
в глазках
           пряча
                 торжество
говорили:
«На!
Бери!
Вот —
      полцарства моего..
Листья
       рушатся с берез.
Дождь
прогноз опроверг...
Половинчатый
             вопрос.
Половинчатый
             ответ...
Посредине тишины
свет мерцает
голубой...
Половинчат
           серп
                луны.
Половинчата
любовь...
Вот и ливень
             отгремел.

Halves

Tsars,
        their wisdom
                    in their seats,
had enough
            but craved for more.
Sly-tongued schemers,
                    they would bleat
"Half my kingdom
                will be yours!"
Half a question,
half a sigh....
Falling leaves
            and falling rain.
Half an answer...
                    Clouds on high,
Weather forecast
wrong again!
In the quiet
of the night
dim blue rays
            like shadows fall....
Half a moon
sheds half a light,
half a love,
        no light at all.

Капля круглая
слышна...
Непонятность
                полусна.
Осторожность
                полумер.
Половинчатость в душе
не дразни,
не вороши.
Шаг один —
                и вот уже
полуправда
лучше лжи!
И уже приятен
                миф.
И верны
полудрузья...
В этот
неизбежный мир
как-то постучался
                я!

Не бояться
длинных гроз,
нянчить время
                на руках
В полный голос!
В полный
                рост!
Или —
        в полный,
или —
никак!

With the passing
of a storm
raindrops gleam
like sparkling beads.
Half-dreams
                    are
                        of fancy born,
prudent minds
                    half-measures breed.

Fickle hearts
Deception screen.
Leave them be
if you are wise.
Just a step,
            and half-truths
                            seem
better,
healthier
than lies.
When a myth
                erases fact,
Half a friend's a friend,
                            and more.

One fine day
I loudly knocked
at the planet's
                fateful door.
  Fear no storm,
  no gloomy night;
  cradling time,
                in life rejoice.

  Stretch up to full,
                    to towering height!
  Speak out in full,
                    in thunderous voice!

Translated by Irina Zheleznova

Лучевая болезнь

Лучевая — так лучевая!
По попробуй
                себя
                        утешь:
слишком долгое
врачевание
и почти никаких
надежд.
Приговоры медиков
                        святы,
снисхождения
не проси...
Только в чем они
                        виновать
внуки
пепельных
                Хиросим?..
Ядовито сверкают
росы.
Притворился чистым
                озон.
И кричат по земле
уродцы,
отвечающие
за отцов!..
Время
        нашу планету
                крутит

Radiation Sickness

Radiation sickness!
                Humanity
puts it bluntly:
                    learn to endure.
The treatment
Takes an eternity,
and there's little chance
of a cure.
Judgement's passed.
No hope,
not a glimmer.
Is it fair—
                come, speak up and say—
that the heirs
of the Hiroshimas
for their fathers
                are made to pay?...
Drops of dew
have a poisonous glitter,
and the air
pretends to be clean.
The complaints
                of the guiltless
                    are bitter
malformed infants
moan and scream.
Mauled by time,
                our ancient planet
is a gaping wound.

Вся она —
как свежий порез...
Ах, какие протяжные

                        руки
у тебя,
лучевая болезнь!
Календарь

            усмехается криво,
опадают
его листы.
Сколько лет

        прошумело со взрыва!
Сколько лет прогудело!
А ты
Влазишь в каждого

                    от рождения
начинаешься
с самых корней.
Как безмолвная

                    эпидемия,
как проклятье
далеких
дней.
Видишь:

            это твои
                        болячки!
Это все еще жалишь
ты —
лучевая болезнь

                        боязни,
фанфаронства
и клеветы.
Это — факт!
Это мне

            не кажется.
Можешь даже
не отвечать...
Погляди,

            как безусо
                        ханжество,
значит, снова
твоя печать!

You are
omnipresent,
                and many-handed,
radiation sickness;
                    your scars
never heal.
Look!
    The calendar, grinning crookedly,
sheds its sheets....
                    The deadly blast
fades away with the years,
                        but, wickedly,
time itself
you seek
to outlast.
In our blood-stream you rove,
                            sowing panic
to our marrow
                you eat
                    your way,
like the germ
of an epidemic,
like the curse
of a blighted day.
You attack us in secret.
                        Your villainy,
like your sores,
is not pretty to see,
radiation sickness
                    of calumny
swagger,
cowardice, spiteful glee!
It's a fact,
            not a fruit of fantasy,
I am not
        sending words
                    down the drain.
Look how beardless
                these days
                        is hypocrisy:
it's a sign
you've cropped up again!

Лучевая болезнь,
                       лучевая
притаившаяся
беда.
Не помогут
             увещевания,
чтоб исчезла ты
навсегда.
И таких докторов
                    не выучит
И таких лекарств
                    не достать
Время вылечит.
Время
       вылечит,
Жаль,
       что долго придется
ждать.

Radiation sickness—
>how lavishly
You bestow your bounty.
>Alas!
Exhortations won't help
>to banish you
from the planet's
tormented face.
There's no drug
in the medical cabinet,
there's no doctor
>to spell your doom.
Time will kill you
>in time.
That's definite.
It's a pity
it won't be soon.

Translated by Irina Zheleznova

Maxim Rylsky (1895-1964) was a major Ukrainian poet. He began writing poetry as a schoolboy, and his first book "On White Islands" was published in 1910 when he was only 15. His artistic tastes became defined at a very early age; he was in love with the 19th century classics, and there were three names he particularly revered: Pushkin, Taras Shevchenko and Adam Mickiewicz. As a child he lived for a time in the family of the famous Ukrainian composer Lysenko, to whom he owes his love for folk songs which he carried through life with him. Maxim Rylsky's songful lyricism is astutely psychological, his hues are reminiscent of a delicate water-colour and his picturesque descriptions are vivid and evocative. He was also an unsurpassed master of translation into Ukrainian and translated, besides the masterpieces of Russian and Polish poetry, such works as Boileau's "Poetic Art", Corneille's and Racine's tragedies and Voltaire's "Pucelle". Until his death he carried on important research at the Kiev Academy of Sciences. Maxim Rylsky was awarded the Lenin Prize in 1960.

MAXIM RYLSKY

МАКСИМ РЫЛЬСКИЙ

Кучерская в Ясной Поляне

Тяжелой ночью, пред седым рассветом,
Он, молчаливый, сгорбленный, худой,
В холодную ноябрьскую погоду,
Стеклом коловшую больное сердце,
В оконце кучерской легонько стукнул
И приказал — приказ последний в жизни! —
В семейный выезд, в бричку, запрягать
Коней без шума...
     То была минута,
Когда с самим собою он порвал —
С тем, с Левиным, с аристократом, с графом
С помещиком, с гусарским офицером
И даже с мудрецом яснополянским,
Что жил двойною жизнью, и, восторг
Толстовцев простоватых вызывая,
И праздные суды и пересуды, —
Да, нить порвал последнюю, живую,
Которою еще был связан с прошлым, —
Судья и подсудимый вместе с тем, —
Чтобы уйти скитальцем неизвестным, —
Куда? Он ясно понимал ли сам?
Глухой проселок, брызги от колес,
Пот лошадиный, бледный луч рассвета,
И крохотная станция, и поезд,
Нестройных мыслей рой, как в тяжком сне,
Шум разговоров, слышный как сквозь воду,
Объятья ненавистной лихорадки —
И смерть...

Coachman's Cottage, Yasnaya Polyana

One heavy night, before a hoary dawn,
In silence, worn and bent with ague and age,
One heavy night in bleak November
That wounds an old man's heart like splintered glass,
He knocked at the coachman's cottage and he ordered—
The one last order to be given in his life—
The coach to be prepared, the horses harnessed,
And, mind, no noise....

It was upon that night

He meant to break forever with himself,
With Levin, the aristocrat, the count,
The country gentleman, the hussar officer,
And even with the legendary sage,
Him who had led a double life, yet caused
The wide-eyed adulation of Tolstoyans
Along with empty gossip and wild cant....
To break the last, the only living·thread
(Accused and stern accuser—all in one)
And leave, and go, a wanderer unknown—
Where to—had he himself a clear idea?
A shadowed country lane; mud splashing from the
wheels

The sweat of horses; faint and pallid dawn.
And then the tiny station, and the train.
His thoughts, confused as in a haunting nightmare;
The fever-deadened hum of conversation,
The hot embraces of the hated ague,
And death....

И в воду синего пруда,
Где он порой с крестьянскими детьми
Купался, бросилась вдова, рыдая,
И не могла прийти в себя, когда
Ее спасли — с какою целью? Кто?

Россия содрогнулась. Вместе с ней
Весь мир.
     Та худощавая рука,
Что ночью постучалась в кучерскую,
Во все живые стукнула сердца
И пробудила светлую тревогу, —
И перед человечества судом,
Как перед совестью своей, предстал он
И суд тот взвесил все его дела,
Искания, сомнения, порывы, —
И приговор был мертвому: бессмертье.

And then into the blue peace of the pond
Where erewhile he had bathed with peasant children
The widow, sobbing wildly, cast herself,
Unable to recover from the shock
When saved—by whom, and why, and to what end?
All Russia shuddered at the tidings, and with her
The entire world.
                         The old man's wizened hand
Which had been knocking at the doors of coachman's
                                              cottage,
Awoke alarm within the hearts of all alive.
At last, before his one and only judge—before
                                        humanity
He stood as though before his own sick conscience.
That judge supreme weighed all his deeds and thoughts,
His search for truth, his doubts, his aspirations:
The sentence which he passed was immortality.

Translated by Dorian Rottenberg

Война алой и белой розы

Был теплый дождь, в траве
стоит вода

ИВ. БУНИН

Был теплый дождь, в траве стоит вода
И стрекоза на ветке обсыхает.
Запах острее донник. Из гнезда
Впервые в небо ласточка взмывает.

Подвязывая светлый виноград,
Смеется девушка сама с собою,
И ярко маки алые горят,
Омыты свежей влагой дождевою.

За речкой песня вдалеке слышна,
А у веранды, здесь, на клумбе малой
Идет в тиши бескровная война,
Все та же: белой розы с розой алой.

The War of the Roses

Warm rain has soaked the
lawn from hedge to hedge

I. BUNIN

Warm rain has soaked the lawn from hedge to hedge
Perched on a twig, the dragonfly sits drying.
Sweet smells the grass. A swallow not long fledged
Starts from the nest to try its wings in flying.

A farmgirl binds her grapevines to their props
And softly laughs—at what? Need we explain?
Crimson, the poppies shine like red wine-drops
Distilled from sunshine, happiness and rain.

Songs float to me from far beyond the river,
While here, beneath the porch, a welcome sight,
A bloodless war seems going on forever:
The war between the red rose and the white.

Translated by Dorian Rottenberg

Mikhail Svetlov (1903-1965) was born in the south of Russia into a poor Jewish family. He moved to Moscow as a young man and there joined a literary group known as "Komsomol Poets". His "Grenada" (1926), which was Mayakovsky's favourite poem, is known to all. It expresses in a most natural way the feeling of international brotherhood which was shared by the people who made the Great October revolution.

Svetlov's poetry emanates gentleness and kindness, and displays a fine sense of humour. He was a romantic, and was prone to poetise everything that surrounded him. His plays in verse: "Fairy Tale", "Twenty Years Later", "The Brandenburg Gate" and others made what we now call the "Svetlov Theatre". His last and fullest collections were "Horizon" (1958), "Hunting Lodge" (1964), and "Poetry of Recent Years", for which he was posthumously awarded the Lenin Prize.

MIKHAIL SVETLOV

МИХАИЛ СВЕТЛОВ

Бессмертие

Как мальчики, мечтая о победах,
Умчались в неизвестные края
Два ангела на двух велосипедах —
Любовь моя и молодость моя.

Иду по следу. Трассу изучаю.
Здесь шина выдохлась, а здесь прокол,
А здесь подъем — здесь юность излучает
День моего вступленья в комсомол.

И, к будущему выходя навстречу,
Я прошлого не скидываю с плеч.
Жизнь не река, она — противоречье,
Она, как речь, должна предостеречь —

Для поколенья, не для населенья,
Как золото, минуты собирай,
И полновесный рубль стихотворенья
На гривенники ты не разменяй.

Не мелочью плати своей отчизне,
В ногах ее не путайся в пути
И за колючей проволокой жизни
Бессмертие поэта обрети.

Не бойся старости. Что седина? — пустое!
Бросайся, рассекай водоворот,
И смерть к тебе не страшною — простою,
Застенчивою девочкой придет.

Immortality

Romantic youngsters, drunk with dreams of triumph,
They've pedalled off to continents unknown,
Two angels on two bicycles fast-flying—
My love and youth, and left me all alone.

And now I'm trying to retrace their route
With here a punctured tire and there a fall....
But steady! Here's a steep ascent—the date
That made me member of the Komsomol.

Nay, when I sally forth toward the future
I won't discard the past as a thing outworn.
What? Life's a river? No, it's all a-quiver
With contradiction, whose main purpose is to warn:

For your generation—not for numeration
Hoard up your minutes as you'd hoard up gold.
But don't exchange the sterling of your talent
For jingling coin that soon grows stale and old.

Don't pay your country back with petty pence,
Don't be a nuisance to her on her course.
And then, when you have cleared life's barbed wire
fence,

A poet's immortality is yours.

Don't fear old age. What's greying hair? Mere trifles
Plunge headlong in, cut straight across the whirl,
And death will come to you, no grisly idol,
But just a blushing sixteen-year-old girl.

Как прожил ты? Что сотворил? Не помнишь?
И всё же ты недаром прожил век.
Твои стихи, тебя зовет на помощь
Тебя похоронивший человек.

Не родственник, ты был ему родимым.
Он будет продолжать с тобой дружить
Всю жизнь, и потому необходимо
Еще настойчивей, еще упрямей жить.

И, новый день встречая добрым взглядом,
Брось неподвижность и, откинув страх,
Поэзию встречай с эпохой рядом
На всем бегу,
На всем скаку,
На всех парах.

И вспоминая молодость былую,
Я покидаю должность старика,
И юности румяная щека
Передо мной опять для поцелуя.

What have you lived for? What have you created?
You can't recall? And yet you haven't lived in vain,
For he who buries you will call you to the rescue—
You and your poetry—again and yet again.

Although no kinsmen, your two spirits are akin.
Such bonds as these survive the grimmest death.
And therefore you must go through thick and thin
And live, live on while able to draw breath.

Yes, greeting the new day with kindly eye,
Cast off your numbness and, discarding fear,
Come out to meet your poetry, your time
Full speed, full steam ahead, in full career!

So, reassured once more, dispelling doubt,
I leave the dismal office of old man,
And once again the sweet lass Youth holds out
Her rosy cheek, which if I want to kiss, I can.

Translated by Dorian Rottenberg

Горизонт

Там, где небо встретилось
с землей,
Горизонт родился молодой.
Я бегу, желанием гоним.
Горизонт отходит. Я за ним.
Вон он за горой, а вот — за морем
Ладно, ладно, мы еще поспорим!
Я в погоне этой не устану,
Мне здоровья своего не жаль,
Будь я проклят, если не достану
Эту убегающую даль!
Все деревья заберу оттуда,
Где живет непойманное чудо,
Всех зверей мгновенно приручу...
Это будет, если я хочу!
Я пущусь на хитрость, на обман,
Сбоку подкрадусь... Но как обидно
На пути моем встает туман,
И опять мне ничего не видно.
Я взнуздал отличного коня —
Горизонт уходит от меня.
Я перескочил в автомобиль —
Горизонта нет, а только пыль.
Я купил билет на самолет.
Он теперь, наверно, не уйдет!
Ровно, преданно гудят моторы.
Горизонта нет, но есть просторы!

Horizon

The sky, it's said, came down to meet the earth
And so, it's said, Horizon came to birth.
This son of Earth and Sky I swore to find:
I ran... he ran... and left me far behind.

Ah well, I thought, this rascal's hard to catch,
But one fine day he's going to find his match.

I see now how he slips from place to place,
From ridge to farther ridge as I pursue;
So I must spare no pains and speed my pace,
And, if I fail, begin the chase anew.

I'll leave my mark in that Horizon-land,
Cut down those ever-beckoning skyline trees,
And tame his beasts to eat out of my hand....
But ever to new boundaries he flies.

On foot, I find, I cannot match his speed;
I saddle up and mount a doughty steed;
Horizon treats this challenge with disdain....
From horse to car I change, but still in vain.
From car to plane—and in the sky I vow
This son of Sky will not escape me now!

But in the air the situation changes:
Where is the skyline to these mountain ranges?

Есть поля, готовые для хлеба,
Есть еще не узнанное небо,
Есть желание! И будь благословенна
Этой каждой дали перемена!..
Горизонт мой! Ты опять далек?
Ну еще, еще, еще рывок!
Как преступник среди бела дня,
Горизонт уходит от меня!
Горизонт мой... Я ищу твой след,
Я ловлю обманчивый изгиб.
Может быть, тебя и вовсе нет?
Может быть, ты на войне погиб?
Мы — мои товарищи и я —
Открываем новые края.
С горечью я чувствую теперь,
Сколько было на пути потерь!
И пускай поднялись обелиски
Над людьми, погибшими в пути , —
Всё далекое ты сделай близким,
Чтоб опять к далекому идти!

Beneath my eyes in swift succession flowing
Are forests, lakes, fields ready for the sowing.
A wealth of scenes for me to feast my eyes on.
But where, oh where's this runaway horizon?

However fast I run or ride or fly,
Your swift retreat keeps pace with my advance;
Whatever speed I set or trick I try,
You still keep leading me a merry dance....

Horizon, you have gone without a trace.
Perhaps you never had a real existence.
But one good thing I brought back from the chase—
A lesson in endurance and persistence.

My friends and I, exploring far and wide,
Keep opening new horizons, rich and real,
And when we hear of any paths untried,
Again we'll show our courage and our zeal.

Despite all losses, bitter though they are,
We'll bring them nearer, goals that are still far!

Translated by Archie Johnstone

В больнице

Ну на что рассчитывать еще-то?
Каждый день встречают, провожают
Кажется, меня уже почетом,
Как селедку луком, окружают.

Неужели мы безмолвны будем,
Как в часы ночные учрежденье?
Может быть, уже не слышно людям
Позвоночного столба гуденье?

Черта с два, рассветы впереди!
Пусть мой пыл как будто остывает,
Всё же сердце у меня в груди
Маленьким боксером проживает.

Разве мы проститься захотели,
Разве «Аллилуйя» мы споем,
Если все мои сосуды в теле
Красным переполнены вином?

Всё мое со мною рядом, тут,
Мне молчать года не позволяют.
Воины с винтовками идут,
Матери с детишками гуляют.

И пускай рядами фонарей
Ночь несет дежурство над больницей
Ну-ка, утро, наступай скорей,
Стань, мое окно, моей бойницей!

In Hospital

What on earth is there to hope for or expect?
Every day they see me off and meet me.
They're surrounding me with honour and respect
Like a fish with onions, nice and neatly.

Are we really doomed to silent gloom,
Like an office left and closed at five?
Will men no longer hear my heart-beats boom,
Signalling that I am still alive?

Damn it, no! There's still some dawns ahead.
Though it looks my gumption's cooling off,
Yet that little boxer in my chest
Doubtless, still sounds militant enough!

What is all this junk about farewell?
What mention can there be of alleluia
When with reddest wine my vessels swell?
Talk of death when life goes surging through you!

All my fire lives on in me unstified
And the times command I have my say—
Soldiers march along with shouldered rifles,
Mothers bring their children out to play.

Let old warden Night be keeping vigil
Over me, this hospital, this gloom...
Come on, morning, quick—I'll make a gunhole
Of the window in my lonely room!

Translated by Dorian Rottenberg

Paruir Sevak. (b. 1924) is a gifted Armenian poet. He was educated at the Gorky Literary Institute. In his poetry he has combined the traditions of ancient Armenian, modern Russian and West-European art. In spite of his great erudition Sevak does not indulge in euphuistic intellectualism. On the contrary, his poetry is firmly rooted in real life. Paruir Sevak is both an excellent craftsman and a true artist.

PARUIR SEVAK

ПАРУЙР СЕВАК

Родине

О родина!
Уже лет тридцать учу я твоії язык,
но все же говорить с тобою о тебе
я без ошибок не могу —
всегда, всегда
сбиваюсь и теряюсь от волненья!

Когда весною ранней
твоей кукушки слышу кукованье,
то мнится,
что кукушка, заикаясь,
мое косноязычье переводит,
восторг телячий мой,
что поздравляет за меня
                    ликующая птица
тебя с твоей весной!

И даже тени летние твои
мои признания безмолвно переводят
и солнцу твоему на синем небосводе
поют хвалебный гимн любви,
то удлиняясь, то сжимаясь,
подобно черным языкам огня...

Когда плоды твои в садах осенних
с деревьев каплями катятся огневыми,
понятно каждому, что это
мое торжественное песнопенье,
дарами вдохновленное твоими.

To My Motherland

O Motherland!
For thirty years I have been striving after
perfection in Thy tongue, but cannot speak
to Thee without mistakes....
Again, again,
emotion makes me lose the thread and stammer

And when, in early Spring,
I hear Thy cuckoos calling
it strikes me
that the stuttering of the cuckoo
translates my tongue-tied utterance,
my fond, dumb ardour,
that the ecstatic bird brings Thee my greetings,
sings of Thy Spring to Thee!

And even silent Summer shadows
translate my wordless declarations
and chant adoring hymns of praise
to Thy Sun in Thine azure heaven,
now stretching long, now falling short,
like murky tongues of flame.

When, in Thy Autumn gardens,
fiery drops from all the trees are falling,
then all men recognise in this
my solemn psalmody's triumphant song,
inspired by Thy good and gracious gifts.

Об этом говорит и твой морозный снег,
он запах детства дальнего принес,
он, как и я, в тебя влюблен навек,
и, словно я, он безголос!..

А в мир,
когда с тобою о тебе я говорю, —
о, даже и тогда
не что иное я творю,
как измеряю скудными словами
молчание мое,
чтоб с болью убедиться снова
в бессильи собственного слова,
в могуществе молчанья твоего...

О кровная!
Ты — многовековая фамилия моя.
А я...
Суметь бы так мне жить,
чтобы тебе стыда не знать
за то, что ты дала мне имя!..
Ведь гибель праведная — жизни половина
Суметь бы так мне умереть,
чтоб ты... оплакивала сына!

Thy frosty snow, too, speaks of this for me.
It brings the scent of childhood's far-off days
like me, eternally in love with Thee
and, like me, voiceless in Thy praise.

Here, too,
where I do speak to Thee of Thee,
why, even here,
all that I have achieved
is to measure with inadequate words
the silence which is mine,
only to realise painfully again
how powerless is my poetic strain,
how mighty is the silence which is Thine.

Blood of my blood!
Thou art Thyself my surname, old and proud,
Whilst I...
so long as I have breath
must live so that no shame
should touch Thee from that name
by Thee on me bestowed!
A good death died—and half of life is won!
And I ...
I would that I die such a death
that Thou... shouldst mourn a son.

Translated by Avril Pyman

Верится мне...

Моя голова
в твоих горячих ладонях,
моя голова
на твоих пахучих коленях.
Не помню,
не вспоминаю
ни о чем, ни о ком,
просто я понимаю
мировой закон:
есть в бескрайней вселенной
просторы планет таких,
где нет ни земных тяготений
ни тягот земных.

My Belief

At times when my head
is cradled in the hot palms of your hands,
At times when my head
is laid in the scented sweetness of your lap
I do not mind
nor call to mind
anything, anyone.
It is simply that my mind
is utterly, wholly won
to the belief that in Infinity
some planets whirl and swirl
as free of our laws of gravity
as of the grave cares of the World.

Translated by Avril Pyman

*Ilya Selvinsky (1899-1968) was born in the Crimea.
When the Civil War began, he joined a revolutionary
detachment fighting the Whites, was captured and put
in prison. After the Civil War was over, Selvinsky
plunged headlong into the mainstream of life. He
worked as an unskilled labourer, a sailor, a stevedore, to
name but a few of his different jobs, and at the same
time managed to study at the Law Department of Mos-
cow University. He had already written some poetry,
and being a man of enormous energy and extremely
lively temperament kept experimenting with forms
and styles. In the 1920s he headed the constructivist
school, proclaimed a manifesto, and revived the genre
of tragedy in verse, writing about a dozen plays, sever-
al of which have been produced on the Soviet stage.
An original lyricist, Selvinsky evolved his own system
of ".beats" in poetry, and introduced new rhythms and
idioms. He has written many verses about animals,
describing their characters, movements and distinctive
traits with competence and not infrequently drawing a
paradoxical parallel between these beasts and men.
His philosophical and love poems of recent years
throb with a thirst for life; they speak of the destructive
power of time and the eternity of Nature.*

ILYA SELVINSKY

ИЛЬЯ СЕЛЬВИНСКИЙ

Тигр

Обдымленный, но избежавший казни,
Дыша боками, вышел из тайги.
Зеленой гривой[1] он повел шаги.
Заиндевевший. Жесткий. Медно-красный.

Угрюмо горбясь, огибает падь,
Всем телом зацадая меж лопаток,
Взлетает без разбега на распадок
и в чащу возвращается опять.

Он забирает запахи до плеч.
Рычит —
            не отзывается тигрица...
И снова в путь. Быть может, под картечь
Теперь уж незачем ему таиться.

Вокруг поблескивание слюды.
Пунцовой клюквы жуткие накраны...
И вдруг — следы! Тигриные следы!
Такие дорогие сердцу лапы...

Они вдоль гривы огибают падь,
И, словно здесь для всех один порядок,
Взлетают без разбега на распадок,
И в чащу возвращаются опять.

---

[1] Опушка тайги.

Tiger

By retribution scorched, from fate he fled.
Through forest brakes with heaving flanks he races.
Towards the green of glades he turns his paces...,
His coat befrosted. Hard. Deep copper-red.

He skirts the gully, muscles hunched, morose.
His pendant body weighs on shoulder-blades.
With ease he leaps the trunks that block the
glades,
Again to seek the forest dark and close.

He fills his lungs. His nostrils scent the air.
He roars
but hears no tigress call a lover....
Then on again. For guns he has no care.
No longer does he deign to lurk in cover.

Small sun-lit mica points gleam all around.
Like spattered blood-drops cranberries dot the
clearing
A sudden halt—fresh foot-prints he has found!
Ah! Tigress-paws, so feline, near, endearing!!

He skirts the gully, drawn by that fresh track
As if some law imposed and all obeyed.
With ease he clears the trunks that block the glade,
Again the virgin forest beckons back....

413

А он — по ним! Гигантскими прыжками
Веселый, молодой не по летам!
Но невдомек летящему, как пламя,
Что он несется по своим следам.

A dashing flame—gigantic leaps and bounds—
Ecstatic   joy returns from far-off youth.
No inkling prompts that brain to sense the truth—
Those prints he left when first he made his rounds.

Translated by Tom Botting

Береза

Березка в розоватой коже
Стоит, сережками струясь.
А на березке — темный глаз,
На око девичье похожий.
Однажды, перейдя межу,
Я шел по молодому лугу,
Но увидал, но подхожу —
И мы глядим в глаза друг другу.
Она как будто вся горит,
Как бы испытывает: струшу?
Заглядывает прямо в душу
И... только что не говорит.
И — черт возьми! — не знаю сам
По я подпал под обаянье
Простого дерева. Глазам
Березки этой изваянье
Предстало, точно древний рок.
Так женственно сияло тело.
Так горестно она глядела,
И был в зрачке такой упрек,
Что я смутился и пойти
Решил не лугом, а деревней,
Как будто встретился в пути
С завороженною царевной.

The Birch-Tree

The birch-tree glitters, catkin-laden,
Bejewelled, in her blushing bark,
And the birch-tree's eye is dark
As the eye of some fair maiden.
Once, as I was passing by
Across the freshly sprouting green,
Enthralled by something I had seen
I went up close and caught her eye....
And she seemed all afire to reach
My inmost heart, as though to test
My courage for some dangerous quest —
She only lacked the gift of speech.
The devil knows — I know not how —
But somehow, spellbound and ensnared
By a mere tree, I hardly dared
To tear my eyes from branch and bough
And so compelling was her look,
So feminine her body gleamed,
So fatal and so sad she seemed,
And in her eyes such mute rebuke,
That I felt guilty and confess
I fled the green and took the street
As though indeed I'd chanced to meet
With some enchanted fair princess.

Translated by Avril Pyman

Трагедия

Говорят, что композитор слышит
На три сотни звуков больше нас.
Но они безмолвствуют иль свищут
Кляксами на ноты устремясь.

Может быть, трагедия поэта
В том, что основное не далось:
Он поет, как птица, но при этом
Слышит, как скрипит земная ось.

Tragedy

People say that the composer's ear
Can catch three-hundred half-tones more than ours.
He cannot reproduce these sounds he hears,
Just whistle—and make inkblots on his scores.

This insufficiency of sounds and words
Makes tragedy, too, of the poet's practice.
For, even while he carols like a bird,
He hears the Earth turn groaning on her axis.

Translated by Avril Pyman

Прелюд

Вот она, моя тихая пристань
Берег письменного стола...

Шел я в жизни, бывало, на приступ
Прогорал на этом дотла.
Сколько падал я, подымался,
Сколько ребер отбито в боях!
До звериного воя влюблялся,
Ненавидел до боли в зубах.
В обличении лживых «истин»
Сколько глупостей делал подчас —
И без сердца на тихую пристань
Возвращался, тоске подчиняясь.

Тихо-тихо идут часы,
За секундой секунду чеканя,
Четвертушки бумаги чисты.
Перья
      дремлют
           в стакане.
Как спокойно. Как хорошо.
Взял перо я для тихого слова...
Но как будто
        я поднял
             ружье:
Снова пламя! Видения снова!
И опять штормовые дела —
В тихой комнате буря да клики...

Берег письменного стола.
Океан за ним — тихий. Великий.

Prelude

Here is my quiet, pacific harbour,
My writing-table's sheltering shore...

Life has left ashes of my ardour
In many a strenuous private war.
I've learnt to fall, get up, go on,
And take the rough in with the smooth,
I loved, and felt like baying at the moon
And hatred gnawed me like a tooth.
Arrayed in foolish Quixote's armour
I've fought false values as my foes —
Then sought out my pacific harbour,
A quiet refuge for my woes.

Tick-tock, tick-tock, the seconds' flight
Is marked by the slow minute hand
The quarto-sheets are virgin white
The pens
      are dozing
            in their stand.
How peacefully the seconds run.
Pacifically, I take my pen...
It is as though
         I'd raised
              a gun:

The flames, the visions come again!
The gale blows lusty as before,
Again, it's "all hands to the mast!"
Beyond my writing table's shore
The Ocean lies — Pacific. Vast.

Translated by Avril Pyman

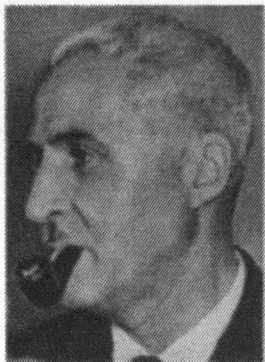

Konstantin Simonov (b. 1915) is a well-known poet, novelist, playwright and publicist. For his work in various genres he has been awarded seven State Prizes. He does not write as much poetry nowadays, but in the 1940s he was probably the best loved poet in the Soviet Union. His wartime poem "Wait For Me"—a passionate invocation for faith and hope—enjoyed truly nationwide popularity. Simonov's lyricism is always topical, vividly expressive and extremely evocative. His most important books of verse are "With You and Without You" (1940), "Friends and Enemies" (1947) and "Poetry" (1954).

KONSTANTIN SIMONOV

КОНСТАНТИН СИМОНОВ

Три стихотворения

Памяти Бориса Горбатова

1

Умер друг у меня — вот какая беда...
Как мне быть — не могу и ума приложить.
Я не думал, не верил, не ждал никогда,
Что без этого друга придется мне жить.
Был в отъезде, когда схоронили его.
В день прощанья у гроба не смог постоять.
А теперь вот приеду — и нет ничего;
Нет его. Нет совсем. Нет. Нигде не видать.
На квартиру пойду к нему — там его нет.
Есть та улица, дом, есть подъезд тот и дверь,
Есть дощечка, где имя его — и теперь.
Есть на вешалке палка его и пальто,
Есть налево за дверью его кабинет...
Все тут есть. Только все это вовсе не то,
Потому что он был, а теперь его нет!
Раньше как говорили друг другу мы с ним?
Говорили: «Споем», «Посидим», «Позвоним»,
Говорили: «Скажи», говорили: «Прочти»,
Говорили: «Зайди ко мне завтра к пяти».
А теперь привыкать надо к слову: «Он был».
Привыкать говорить про него: «Говорил»,
Говорил, приходил, помогал, выручал,
Чтобы я не грустил — долго жить обещал.
Еще в памяти все твои живы черты,
А уже не могу я сказать тебе «ты».
Говорят: раз ты умер — таков уж закон, —
Вместо «ты» про тебя говорить надо: «он»,

Three Poems

To the memory of Boris Gorbatov

1.

My dear friend is deceased—I am stunned with the grief.
And what am I to do, now my dear friend is gone?
Never thought, never dreamed and would never believe
That without my dear friend I would have to live on.
I was gone, when they took him away on a pall,
And the funeral rites were performed without me.
And when now I'll return, there'll be nothing at all:
There'll be nothing to hear, there'll be nothing to see.
When I go to his home, he'll no longer be there.
There's the street and the house, and the very same door,
And the plate with his name on the door, as before.
There's the rack that still carries his hat and his cane
And the study where he over books used to pore.
There is everything still—but no longer the same,
Because then he was here, whereas now, he's no more!
What before were the words to each other we spoke?
"Let us sit down and talk, sing a song, have a smoke,"
We would say: "I would like you to go through this book,"
Or: "Come over tomorrow, and we'll have a look."
But now I'm to live with the fact that he's dead
And get used to pronouncing the words: "He once said."
He had said, he had helped, he had followed along,
And to cheer me, he promised that he would live long.
In my mind I still see the dear features I knew,
But no more, as before, can I say to him, "You".
But they say, since one's dead that's the way it must be—
I'll no longer say "you", I shall have to say "he".

Вместо слов, что люблю тебя, надо: «любил»,
Вместо слов, что есть друг у меня, надо: «был».
Так ли это? Не знаю. По-моему — нет!
Свет погасшей звезды еще тысячу лет
К нам доходит. А что ей, звезде, до людей?
Ты добрей был её, и теплей, и светлей,
Да и срок невелик — тыщу лет мне не жить,
На мой век тебя хватит — мне по дружбе светить

2

Умер молча, сразу, как от пули,
Побледнев, лежит — уже ничей.
И стоят в почетном карауле
Четверо немолодых людей.

Четверо, не верящие в бога,
Провожают раз и навсегда
Пятого в последнюю дорогу,
Зная, что не встретят никогда.

А в глазах — такое выраженье,
Словно верят, что еще спасут,
Словно в год войны из окруженья,
На шинель подняв, его несут.

3

Дружба настоящая не старится,
За небо ветвями не цепляется, —
Если уж приходит срок, так валится
С грохотом, как дубу полагается.
От ветров при жизни не качается,
Смертью одного из двух кончается.

And instead of "I love you", "I loved you" must say
Not "I have a good friend", but "I had one, one day"
Is this so? I'm not sure, for all wrong it appears.
When a star has gone out, for a thousand more years
People here on the Earth see the light of that star.
You are warmer and brighter by far than a star,
And a short time will pass till in coffin I lie,
So for me you will shine till the day that I die.

2.

Death struck swift, and now it seems he's sleeping,
Lying pale, and nobody's today,
And the guard of honour four are keeping,
Four whose youth has somehow slipped away.
Four, for whom there is no heaven or hell,
See the fifth one off, their ranks deplete,
Bid their friend an ultimate farewell,
Knowing that they nevermore shall meet.
Eyes with steadfast resolution staring,
We shall save him yet, they seem to say.
As if on their shoulders they are bearing
A friend, severely wounded in the fray.

3.

Friendship, true, with time does not diminish,
Clutches not at clouds up in the blue;
It just tumbles, when it nears its finish,
With a rumble, just as oak-trees do.
While alive, no wind can ever bend it,
Only death of one of them will end it.

Translated by Eugene Felgenhauer

Boris Slutsky (b. 1919) published his first book of poetry in 1957 when he was almost 40. He is an original poet who sees the truth of the life around him with a rare clarity of vision. He entered the literary scene when Soviet writers were struggling against the practice of embellishing and varnishing the truth and striving to cultivate a sober, realistic attitude to life Slutsky's first poems were about the war. Those collections were entitled "Memory" and "Today and Yesterday". His poetry "Physicists and Lyricists" started off a long and heated discussion, involving readers, critics and the general public, on the role of art in modern society. Slutsky's poetry is frankly polemical, his ideas are clearly formulated (which comes of his being a lawyer, perhaps) and his tone tends to be oratorial. The work of many young poets has been strongly influenced by him. Boris Slutsky is also a well-known translator of Slav poets (Czechs, Serbians and Poles) into Russian.

BORIS SLUTSKY

БОРИС СЛУЦКИЙ

Лошади в океане

И. Эренбургу

Лошади умеют плавать,
Но — не хорошо. Недалеко.

«Глория» — по-русски значит «Слава», —
Это вам запомнится легко.

Шел корабль, своим названьем гордый,
Океан старался превозмочь.

В трюме, добрыми мотая мордами,
Тыща лошадей топталась день и ночь.

Тыща лошадей! Подков четыре тыщи!
Счастья все ж они не принесли.

Мина кораблю пробила днище
Далеко-далёко от земли.

Люди сели в лодки, в шлюпки влезли.
Лошади поплыли просто так.

Как же быть и что же делать, если
Нету мест на лодках и плотах?

Плыл по океану рыжий остров.
В море, в синем, остров плыл гнедой.

И сперва казалось — плавать просто,
Океан казался им рекой.

Horses in the Ocean

To Ilya Ehrenburg

Horses can swim but they don't venture far—
That is a fact, and here is the story:

In times of peace, just after the war,
There was a ship by the name of Gloria.

She was out at sea one fateful day,
Across the ocean ploughing her way.

On the surging waves she tossed and rolled,
A thousand horses locked in her hold.

Four thousand horse-shoes—good luck galore!—
And yet she was never to reach the shore.

For she struck a mine and was badly rent,
And a part of her was twisted and bent.

The life-boats on board, alas, were few;
The life-boats were used to save the crew.

As for the horses, their plight was grim,
For, like it or not, they had to swim.

On and on they swam after the boats,
An island of horses with red-brown coats.

At first they were calm, for they did not dream
That the ocean was anything but a stream.

Но не видно у реки той края.
На исходе лошадиных сил

Вдруг заржали кони, возражая
Тем, кто в океане их топил.

Кони шли на дно и ржали, ржали,
Все на дно покуда не пошли.

Вот и все. А все-таки мне жаль их
Рыжих, не увидевших земли.

But it stretched without end like a wintry night,
And the longed-for land was never in sight.

On their watery way all their strength was spent,
And they whinnied in fear and in wonderment.

They whinnied and neighed and struggled for breath
As down they went to their watery death.

There are things to which one gets resigned,
But those luckless horses prey on my mind.

Translated by Irina Zheleznova

Старух было много...

Старух было много, стариков было мало:

То, что гнуло старух, стариков ломало.

Старики умирали, хватаясь за сердце,

А старухи, рванув гардеробные дверцы,

Доставали костюм выходной, суконный,

Покупали гроб дорогой, дубовый,

И глядели в последний, как лежит

                              законный

Прижимая лацкан рукой пудовой.

Постепенно образовались квартиры,

А потом из них слепились кварталы,

Где одни старухи молитвы твердили,

Боялись воров, о смерти болтали.

Они болтали о смерти, словно

Она с ними чай пила ежедневно,

Такая же тощая, как Анна Петровна,

Такая же грустная, как Марья Андревна.

Вставали рано, словно матросы,

И долго, темные, словно индусы,

Чесали гребнем редкие косы,

Катали в пальцах старые бусы.

There Were Many Old Women

There were many old women and only a few old men...
Perhaps it was life, just life, or perhaps

                        something else again

But it bent the old women, and the old men it broke:
Some died of heart-attacks, others of strokes.
The old women went through their closets

                        and chests,

And laid out their spouses decked in their

                        Sunday best.

The coffins they bought were of oak, and rather

                        expensive,

The hands of the dead looked uncannily massive....
In time, whole housefuls of flats filled slowly with

                        shadows:

Whole blockfuls appeared, whole streetfuls of widows,
Who were fearful of thieves and also of burglars,
Passed yellowish beads between yellowing fingers,
And chatted of death as of a neighbour, or friend
With whom they took tea, and on whom

                        they had learnt to depend

A neighbour or friend as gaunt as poor Anna Petrovna
Of long-faced and sad-eyed as Maria Andrevna.
They rose with the dawn, like sailors at sea,
And for hours on end, being hopelessly free,
Sat in baggy old smocks and shapeless old dresses
Listlessly combing their sparse, thinning tresses.

Ложились рано, словно солдаты,
А спать не спали долго-долго,
Катая в мыслях какие-то даты,
Какие-то вехи любви и долга.
И вся их длинная,
Вся горевая,
Вся их радостная,
Вся трудовая —
Вставала в звонах ночного трамвая
На миг
        бессонницы не прерывая.

To bed they went early, like army recruits,
But sleep would not come, and they lay there, mute,
In their dusty and darkish chambers.
And thought about things that were good to remember.

Their lives rose before them, the toll of love
                         and of duty,
Their long lives of toil, and brief moments of
                             beauty....

The night tram clanged by,
In the sky
The night stars erupted....
Insomnia's vigil
Was uninterrupted.

Translated by Irina Zheleznova

Физики и лирики

Что-то физики в почете.
Что-то лирики в загоне.
Дело не в сухом расчете,
Дело в мировом законе.

Значит, что-то не раскрыли
Мы,
　　　что следовало нам бы!
Значит, слабенькие крылья —
Наши сладенькие ямбы,
И в пегасовом полете
Не взлетают наши кони...
То-то физики в почете,
То-то лирики в загоне.

Это самоочевидно.
Спорить просто бесполезно.
Так что даже не обидно,
А скорее интересно
Наблюдать, как, словно пена
Опадают наши рифмы
И величие
　　　　　　степенно
Отступает в логарифмы.

Physicists and Lyricists

Physicists are held in reverence,
Lyricists—let's be truthful—
                              in the shade.
This is not an ordinary preference,
It's a law, and is as such obeyed.

All it means is that poetic reverie
Sidetracks us from pathways of discovery,
That our verse is so much syrup,
That our feet just miss the stirrup,
That our Pegasus, as has been found,
Merely trots but never leaves the ground.

Physicists deserve the world's esteem,
Lyricists clearly don't, so it would seem.

And it's all so evident and obvious
That to take offence is stupid really.
So, instead of being envious,
Let us watch objectively and coolly
How the foam of measures rhythmic
    Drops away in sheer dejection,
    And the mantle of distinction
    Falls to
                  spirals logarithmic.

Translated by Irina Zheleznova

Yaroslav Smelyakov (b. 1913) devotes all his poetry to the man of toil, a character faithful in friendship, constant in his affections, undaunted by hardships and capable of taking the rough with the smooth. Smelyakov's roughly affectionate manner of speech creates a true-to-life picture of his character. The poet himself is a man of toil. In his lifetime he has had to work as a street-sweeper, boiler-stoker, newspaper reporter, type-setter, miner, etc. He believes in deeds and not in words. He is also a romantic—he loves ballads, and has a talent for creating plots with a strong impact. But whichever genre he writes in Smelyakov is always thrifty with words. His main quality is the ability to find the only correct, and sometimes unexpected, epithet.

YAROSLAV SMELYAKOV

ЯРОСЛАВ СМЕЛЯКОВ

Разговор о поэзии

Ты мне сказал, небрежен и суров,
что у тебя — отрадное явленье! —
есть о любви четыреста стихов,
а у меня два-три стихотворенья.

Что свой талант (а у меня он был,
и, судя по рецензиям, не мелкий)
я чуть не весь, к несчастью, загубил
на разные гражданские подделки.

И выходило — мне резону нет
из этих обличений делать тайну, —
что ты — всепроникающий поэт,
а я — лишь так, ремесленник случайный

Ну что ж, ты прав. В альбомах у девиц
средь милой дребедени и мороки,
в сообществе интимнейших страниц
мои навряд ли попадутся строки.

И вряд ли, что, открыв красиво рот,
когда замолкнут стопки и пластинки,
мой грубый стих томительно споет
плешивый гость притихшей вечеринки.

Помилуй бог! — я вовсе не горжусь,
а говорю не без душевной боли,
что, видимо, не очень-то гожусь
для этакой литературной роли.

Talking of Poetry

In an offhand, uppish way, you said to me
You had four hundred poems about love,
While I—too bad!—had only two or three,
By any standards, plainly not enough.

Yes, all my talent, you went on to add,
(Not insignificant, to judge by the reviews)
Was wasted on all sorts of civic fads—
Rhymed comments to the flow of daily news.

The sum of what you said amounts, in fact,
To stating—and you spared no pains to show it
That I was just a potboiler and hack
And you the genuine, one-and-only master-poet.

Ah, well, there's something to it, I confess.
Among the humdrum stuff in girlish albums—
Ever so intimate—you'll hardly find, I guess
A line of mine, unpolished, crude and callous.

And hardly, coyly opening his lips
When wineglasses and records stop their din,
Will any bald-pate at a party, between sips,
Deign to select a piece of mine to sing.

No, god forbid! There's no offence at all.
It's not without regret that I admit:
For playing such a literary role
Y. Smelyakov is perfectly unfit.

Я не могу писать по пустякам.
как словно бы мальчишка желторотый,
иная есть нелегкая работа,
иное назначение стихам.

Меня к себе единственно влекли —
я только к вам тянулся по наитью,
великие и малые событья
чужих земель и собственной земли.

Не так-то много написал я строк,
не все они удачны и заметны,
радиостудий рядовой пророк,
ремесленник журнальный и газетный.

Мне в общей жизни, в общем, повезло
я знал ее и крупно и подробно.
И рад тому, что это ремесло
созданию истории подобно.

It's not for me to write on themes like the above
I gladly leave it to the younger geneiation,
Preferring subjects not concerned with love;
My poems have a different destination.

The only theme that really drew my soul,
That made me take a pen into my hand
Were the events and facts, both great and small
That make up life in mine and other lands.

It isn't very much that I've composed,
Not all I wrote was really a success.
I am a rank-and-filer, I suppose,
A daily drudger for the radio and press.

Yet all in all, I've been in luck through life,
Known it quite well, in big and small partaking
And so I like my job because it's like
Partly, at least—the job of history-making.

Translated by Dorian Rottenberg

Карман

На будних потертых штанишках
известных окрестным дворам,
у нашего есть у мальчишки
единственный только карман.

По летне-весенним неделям
под небом московским живым
он служит ему и портфелем
и верным мешком вещевым.

Кладет он туда без утайки,
по всем закоулкам гостя,
то круглую темную гайку,
то ржавую шляпку гвоздя.

Какие там к черту игрушки —
подделки ему не нужны.
надежнее комнатной пушки
помятая гильза войны.

И я говорю без обмана,
что вы бы нащупать смогли
в таинственных недрах кармана
ребячую горстку земли.

Ты сам, мальчуган красноротый
в своей разобрался судьбе:
пусть будут земля и работа —
и этого хватит тебе.

The Pocket

There's a brave little soul in this town
Whose trousers have one single pocket,
And I'll try to retell to you now
With what he's accustomed to stock it.

It serves him in summer and spring
As knapsack and satchel combined,
Packed, at first glance, with any old thing
That a curious youngster can find.

Through the neighbourhood daily he roams,
To the onlooker always at leisure,
But in fact it is really for treasure
That the alleys and by-ways he combs.

He doesn't believe in toys;
No artifices for him.
But a crumpled old cartridge enjoys
His favour for no mere whim.

Alongside with nuts and washers
And objects of equal worth
He keeps in that pocket-locker
A sample of simple earth.

With his own hands the red-cheeked youngster
Blueprints his future lot:
Earth and work are the things that matter.
Baubles and toys do not.

Translated by Dorian Rottenberg

Столовая на окраине

Люблю рабочие столовки,
весь их бесхитростный уют,
где руки сильные неловко
из пиджака или спецовки
рубли и трешки достают.

Люблю войти вечерним часом
в мирок, набитый жизнью, тот,
где у окна стеклянной кассы
теснится правильный народ.

Здесь стены вовсе не богаты,
на них ни фресок, ни ковров —
лишь розы плоские в квадратах
полуискусных маляров.

несут в тарелках борщ горячий,
лапша колышется, как зной,
и пляшут гривеннички сдачи
перед буфетчицей одной.

Тут, взяв, что надо из окошка,
отнюдь не кушают — едят,
и гнутся слабенькие ложки
в руках окраинных девчат.

Здесь, обратя друг к дружке лица
нехитрый пробуя салат,
из магазина продавщицы
в халатах синеньких сидят.

Workers' Canteens

I've come to love the homely comfort
Of Moscow's factory canteens
Where big, strong hands pull hard-earned rubles
From jackets, overalls and jeans....

I love to come there of an evening
Into that teeming little world.
And meet before the cashier's window
Men used to matching deed with word.

The whitewashed walls display no splendour—
No frescoes here or costly rugs.
Just quaint, naively painted roses
Reflected in most common mugs.

The soup-plates steam with vermicelli
Or, starry, glint with scalding borsch.
The saucy barmaid clicks her money.
Newcomers trail in from the porch.

They get their food and find a table
To eat—like workers, not like earls.
The tin spoons bend between the fingers
Of muscular suburban girls.

To taste the unassuming salad
Clad in their uniforms of blue,
Gay flocks of dimpled shopgirls hasten
Into those cozy precincts too.

Сюда войдет походкой спорой,
самим собой гордясь в душе,
в таком костюмчике, который
под стать любому атташе,
в унтах, подвернутых как надо,
с румянцем крупным про запас,
рабочий парень из бригады,
что всюду славится сейчас.

Сюда торопятся подростки,
от нетерпенья трепеща,
здесь пахнет хлебом и известкой
здесь дух металла и борща.

Здесь все открыто и понятно,
здесь все отмечено трудом,
мне все близки и все приятны,
и я не лишний за столом.

Occasionally, brisk and breezy,
Proud of his handsome self at heart,
In clothes an attache would envy—
A miracle of tailor's art—

With boots rolled down to flaunt their lining,
A wealth of colour in his cheeks—
Walks in a lad from a team of turners
Grown famous over recent weeks.

Keen youngsters hurry here, all eager
For the impending evening meal.
The place exudes a rich aroma
Of bread and plaster, borsch and steel.

Here minds are frank and hearts are open—
It's you for me and me for you.
I like them all and understand them
And know that I am welcome too.

Translated by Dorian Rottenberg

Alexei Surkov (b. 1899) rightly calls himself a "typical representative of his generation, of those rightless, indigent millions whom the October Revolution which they carried through made into soldiers and builders of communism...". The son of a poor peasant, a veteran of the Civil War, an experienced organiser and orator, Surkov entered Russian poetry as a convinced champion of democratic principles in art. He has waged a constant battle with aesthetes and snobs, he despises the exotic romanticism of fantasy, and believes in the harsh truth of reality.
His wartime poetry is the best known and most popular. For many years Alexei Surkov has been one of the secretaries of the Union of Soviet Writers, and is also a member of the Presidium of the Soviet Peace Council.

ALEXEI SURKOV

АЛЕКСЕЙ СУРКОВ

Ты думаешь, это не страшно было —
Решить, что бога на свете нет,
Что в нашей вселенной иная сила
Заведует ходом звезд и планет?

Ты, может быть, думаешь, было просто,
Как выпить глоток воды из реки,
Душе привычного, среднего роста
Признать себя, всему вопреки?

А это не просто — ночью проснуться
И, видя паденье звезд с высоты,
Познать бесконечность и не ужаснуться
Тому, что в мире пылинка ты.

Не просто прорваться сквозь дым томлений
Тому, кто, жизнь безмерно любя,
Познал, что тысячи поколений
Рождались и умерли раньше тебя.

Не просто знать, беспощадно ясно,
Что смерть придет — и судьба твоя
И все, что в мире было прекрасно,
Угаснет с твоим беспокойным Я;

Что можно жить без аллаха и спаса,
Без райских приманок и адских мук
И, страх пересилив, до смертного часа
Не выпустить душу из собственных рук.

You suppose it wasn't a horror at first
To think there's no god and another force
Exists in the godless universe
To drive the planets along their course?

Maybe you think it was very simple
—simple as drinking a glass of water—
For a soul of medium, average calibre
To acknowledge itself to be mortal?

No, it wasn't easy one day to awake
And watching the stars roll down from their heights
To behold infinity and not to quake
At the thought that we, men, were simply mites!

Not so simple to break through the mist of frustration
For a human, in love with this life and this earth,
Finding out that thousands of generations
Long before him were doomed to death from birth.

No, it wasn't easy to realise
Hard and clear, that you had to die
And all this beauty before your eyes
Would fade together with your restless I,

That life could go on without Allah or Saviour,
Heaven's enticement or Hell's torment,
So just overcome fear of death and brave your
Destiny with your head unbent.

Лишь смело покончив с последней химерой
Сердца леденящей, как холод ночной,
Ты плечи расправишь и полной мерой
Познаешь радость жизни земной.

Слова человеческой песни слыша,
Почувствуешь, зову природы в ответ,
Что люди — хозяева мира и выше
Идеи и силы на свете нет.

Only boldly dispensing with the last of chimeras
That cut through the heart like the blade of a knife,
Can you put back your shoulders and in full measure
Know all the joy of this earthly life.

Hearing a human song resound
You'll understand, stirred by Nature's call:
No higher power or idea can be found:
Man alone is almighty after all.

Translated by Dorian Rottenberg

Мой современник

В вихре дней, что шумят над планетой
Ты проходишь, в легендах воспетый,
Покоритель высот и стремнин,
Солнцем общего счастья согретый —
Коммунист, человек, гражданин.

Верность людям воздвигнув твердыней,
Веря в правду и правду любя,
Ты корыстью, хвальбой и гордыней
Никогда не унизил себя.

Беспокойный, пытливый, горячий,
Не разменивал жизнь на гроши
И друзьям раздавал без отдачи
Золотые запасы души.

Трассу счастья назначив планете,
Перед временем совестью чист,
Ты за все в этом мире в ответе —
Человек, гражданин, коммунист.

Дерзкой волей смиряя упрямо
Своенравного времени бег,
Ты в завещанный Лениным век
Входишь твердо, напористо, прямо —
Гражданин, коммунист, человек.

My Contemporary

With the whirlwind of time, o'er the world as it flies,
You advance, famed in legend and song,
Born to harness the waters and conquer the skies
Man and communist, friend of the good and the wise,
Bitter foe of injustice and wrong.

From beginning to end always true to mankind,
You hold truth to be highest of all.
Neither avarice nor vociferous pride
Ever marred your unwavering soul.

Restless, eager to learn and to act,
Shunning meanness and filth from the start,
You shared with your friends all the treasure you had—
The gold of your generous heart.

With humanity's happiness always in mind,
Clear in conscience before the whole world,
The fortunes, the future, the fate of mankind
In your confident hands you hold.

Bold, determined, you break the resistance
Of the shiftless, the hostile, the cold,
Marching on, despite hardship and distance
To the era that Lenin foretold.

Translated by Dorian Rottenberg

Alexander Tvardovsky (b. 1910) is an outstanding Russian poet to whom clearly apply the words of Belinsky, the great 19th century critic: "The significance of a people's poet depends on how fully his own personality reflects the spirit of the nation." Tvardovsky's genius manifested itself most vividly in his large poems which marked historical milestones in the life of our country: "The Land of Muravia" (collectivisation), "Vasily Terkin" and "Roadside House" (the Great Patriotic War), and "Space Beyond Space" (elimination of the consequences of the Stalin personality cult). Soviet critics have unanimously acclaimed Tvardovsky for the depth of his historical thinking and for the authenticity with which he portrays the spirit of the ordinary people's life.

Alexander Tvardovsky is the chief editor of the literary magazine Novy Mir and a prominent public figure. He was awarded the Lenin Prize in 1961.

ALEXANDER TVARDOVSKY

АЛЕКСАНДР ТВАРДОВСКИЙ

Нет, жизнь меня не обделила,
Добром своим не обошла,
Всего с лихвой дано мне было
В дорогу, — света и тепла.

И сказок в трепетную память,
И песен стороны родной,
И старых праздников с попами,
И новых с музыкой иной.

И в захолустье, потрясенном
Всемирным чудом новых дней —
Старинных зим с певучим стоном
Далеких — за лесом — саней.

И весен в дружном развороте,
Морей и речек на дворе,
Икры лягушечьей в болоте,
Смолы у сосен на коре.

И летних гроз, грибов и ягод,
Росистых троп в траве глухой,
Пастушьих радостей и тягот,
И слез над книгой дорогой.

И ранней горечи и боли,
И детской мстительной мечты,
И дней, не высиженных в школе
И босоты, и наготы.

Life's not been grudging of her treasure
Nor done me out of any right
But given all things in good measure
And set my way with warmth and light.

My memory's a-thrum with stories
And songs of home and village feasts,
New songs to celebrate new victories
And old processionals with priests.

And in our quiet backwood—shaken
By the vast changes of our time—
I've heard the olden Winters waken
The distant sleigh-bells' mournful chime.

Seen swift Springs follow one another,
Whole seas and streams in our backyard,
And frog-spawn on the dark bog-water,
And resin on the pine-tree's bark.

Known summer storms and forest berries,
Mushrooms, grass-tangled paths and brooks
A herd-boy's simple joys and worries
And tears shed over well-loved books.

And early grief and disappointment,
A child's vindictive fantasy,
No shoes for school and I playing truant,
The dismal grind of poverty,

Всего — и скудности унылой
В потемках отчего угла...
Нет, жизнь меня не обделила,
Ничем в ряду не обошла.

Ни щедрой выдачей здоровья
И сил надолго про запас,
Ни первой дружбой и любовью,
Что во второй не встретишь раз.

Ни славы замыслом зеленым —
Отравой сладкой строк и слов,
Ни кружкой с дымным самогоном
В кругу певцов и мудрецов,

Тихонь и спорщиков до страсти,
Чей толк не прост и речь остра
Насчет былой и новой власти,
Насчет добра и недобра...

Чтоб жил и был всегда с народом
Чтоб ведал все, что станет с ним
Не обошла тридцатым годом,
И сорок первым, и иным...

И столько в сердце поместила,
Что диву даться до поры,
Какие резкие под силу
Ему ознобы и жары.

И что мне малые напасти
И незадачи на пути,
Когда я знаю это счастье —
Не мимоходом жизнь пройти.

Не мимоходом стороною
Ее увидеть без хлопот,
Но знать горбом и всей спиною
Ее крутой и жесткий пот.

И будто дело молодое —
Все, что затеял и слепил,

464

And ragged want, excluding pleasure
From my poor native backwood's night...
Life's not been grudging of her treasure
Nor docked me of a single right...

Nor stinted health—a generous helping—
Nor strength to last me in good store,
Nor missed out on first love, first friendship
Two things that come but once—no more.

Nor fame—sweet poison of our pages,
A shifting sand on which to build—
Nor gathering of bards and sages
Round misted mugs of home-distilled.

Inveterate talkers, quiet listeners,
Subtle of tongue and sharp of wit,
Who love to argue moral issues
And history—and politics.

And in the years of Nineteen Thirty
And 'Forty-One I've played my part,
And everything that's touched my country
Has always touched me to the heart.

The wonder is it still keeps going—
Life's filled it full as it can hold
Then laid it bare to great winds blowing
From cold to hot and hot to cold.

But what care I for small misfortunes,
The failures that my way bestrew,
When well I know that true good fortune
Is not to get round life—but through,

Nor be an uninvolved spectator
Who'd ford the stream but not get wet
But, as the way runs steeper, straighter,
To share the burden and the sweat

And think it all beginner's labour
And all one ever shaped or sowed

Считать одной ничтожной долей
Того, что людям должен был.

Зато порукой обоюдной
.Любая скрашена страда.

Еще и впредь мне будет трудно
Но чтобы страшно—никогда.

An insignificant down-payment
On a great debt to others owed.

Where there are helping hands a-plenty
The heaviest work goes merrily.
The way ahead runs none too gently:
But should I fear it then? Not I.

Translated by Avril Pyman

Ты дура, смерть: грозишься людям
Своей бездонной пустотой,
А мы условились, что будем
И за твоею жить чертой.

И за твоею мглой безгласной
Мы — здесь, с живыми заодно.
Мы только врозь тебе подвластны,
Иного смерти не дано.

И, нашей связаны порукой,
Мы вместе знаем чудеса:
Мы слышим в вечности друг друга
И различаем голоса.

И как бы ни был провод тонок,
Между своими связь жива.

Ты это слышишь, друг-потомок?
Ты подтвердишь мои слова?..

Death, you're a fool: you boast and threaten
Us humans with your void forlorn
When we, between ourselves, have settled
That we'll live on beyond your bourn,

Beyond your mute obscurity
We're here—with those that walk the earth...
Singly—we own your sovereignty,
But that is all your empire, Death!

You see, because we stick together,
A miracle has come to be!
And we can recognise each other
As voices in eternity.

However stretched communications
We'll always keep an open line...
Speak, friends of future generations!
Do you confirm these words of mine?

Translated by Avril Pyman

Собратьям по перу

В деле своем без излишней тревоги
Мы затвердили с давнишней поры
То, что горшки обжигают не боги,
Ну, а не боги, так — дуй до горы.

Только по той продвигаясь дороге,
Нам бы вдобавок усвоить пора:
Верно, горшки обжигают не боги,
Но обжигают их — мастера!

To My Colleagues

In our trade we've established in manner explicit
That gods have no part in the firing of pots,
And if not the gods... then the sky is the limit,
Pile on the pressure and blow it up hot!

But it's high time we took this conclusion one further:
True, gods have no part in the firing of pots.
One lesson, however, should lead to another:
Skilled workmen are needed, if gods are not!

Translated by Avril Pyman

Снега потемнеют синие
Вдоль загородных дорог,
И воды зайдут низинами
В прозрачный еще песок.

Недвижной гладью прикинутся
И разом — в сырой ночи́
В поход отовсюду ринутся,
Из русел выбив ручьи.

И, сонная, талая,
Земля обвянет едва,
Листву прошивая старую,
Пойдет строчить трава.

И с ветром нежно-зеленая
Ольховая пыльца,
Из детских лет донесенная,
Как тень, коснется лица.

И сердце почует за́ново,
Что свежесть поры любой
Не только была, да канула,
А есть и будет с тобой.

Blue snow will soon be turning grey
On roadways out beyond the town
The low-lying patches churned away
By waking waters seeping down.

In clear, clean sand and seeming quiet
The waiting waters still lie low;
Then, one wild night, in steaming riot
They'll rise, the streams will overflow.

And as the earth, still all a-mush
A-thaw and sleepy, is drying out
Sprinkling the leaf-mould, with a rush
The new green grass will start to sprout.

Then alder-pollen, drifting green,
Will blow by on the breeze,
Blown up from childhood's distant scene,
Shadow-soft to the cheeks.

And again the heart shall respond enthralled
To the season's freshness, as before,
Not gone, as it seemed, beyond recall,
But with us now—and evermore.

Translated by Avril Pyman

Nikolai Tikhonov (b. 1896) is a poet born of the Revolution, a soldier and traveller. "As a schoolboy of 9 I witnessed Bloody Sunday on January 9, 1905, and as a soldier of 18 I found out what it was like to be in a world war. I joined the Red Army the year it was formed." This autobiographical note explains the militant character of Tikhonov's themes. At the same time he is an active fighter for peace, a member of the World Peace Council, and a tireless advocate of friendship among the nations. How can these two concepts go together? The answer as to how a soldier and a peace champion can be found side by side in one and the same man is given in the poet's own words: "As an old soldier who fought in four wars I could not but join this noble movement for peace...." Tikhonov's clear-cut laconic ballads which brought him renown as early as the 1920s ("The Horde" and "The Home-brew" collections) sing a hymn to strength and courage inspired by justice. Tikhonov is a very keen traveller, and is well known in the Caucasus, Central Asia and the Far East. His translations of Soviet non-Russian poetry are the work of a true master. For his literary and public activities he has been awarded the title of Hero of Socialist Labour.

NIKOLAI TIKHONOV

НИКОЛАЙ ТИХОНОВ

Под сосен снежным серебром,
Под пальмой юга золотого,
Из края в край, из дома в дом
Проходит Ленинское слово.

Уже на дальних берегах,
Уже не в первом поколенье,
Уже на всех материках
И чтут и любят имя: Ленин!

В сердцах народных утвержден,
Во всех краях он стал любимым,
Но есть страна одна, где он
Свой начал путь неповторимый,

Где были ярость, ночь, тоска
И грохот бурь в дороге длинной,
Где он родного языка
Любил могучие глубины,

И необъятный небосклон,
И все растущий вольный ветер...
Любить Россию так, как он, —
Что может быть святей на свете!

Where firs by snow all silvered stand,
Where palms grow in the golden south,
From home to home, from land to land,
His words pass on from mouth to mouth.

On shores both near and far away,
By more than one new generation
In all five continents, today
His name is held in veneration.

He is enthroned in peoples' hearts,
And is beloved in every clime.
In one, though, he commenced his path
Unheard of since the birth of time.

A land where grief and fury reigned,
Where peals of brewing thunder rolled,
And where he loved his native tongue,
Its mines of eloquence untold.

He loved her skies, her steppes so vast,
Her mounting wind of liberty...
What can be nobler than to love
One's native land as Lenin did.

Translated by Louis Zellikoff

Под Ленинградом

Поля, холмы, лощины темно-синие
И перелески легкою волной,
Но через все — невидимая линия,
Неслышная — идет передо мной.

От Ладоги вы всю ее пройдете,
Она к заливу прямо приведет,
На старой карте вы её найдете,
С пометкой грозной — сорок первый год

Та линия ещё сегодня дышит,
Она по сердцу вашему идет,
Она листву вот этих рощ колышет
И в новый дом подчеркивает вход.

Возможно, поколеньям близким
Не так, как будущим, она видна,
Хоть кое-где гранитным обелиском
И надписью отмечена она.

Но, кажется, она еще дымится,
И молнии пронизывают мрак,
На ней, на этой огненной границе,
Отброшен был и остановлен враг.

Заговорила роща на откосе,
Прислушайся, о чем шумит она,
Как будто ветер, набежав, проносит
Бесчисленных героев имена!

Near Leningrad

In peace lie hills and fields and dark-blue valleys,
And woods like lazy billows rise and fall;
Yet still before me, tortuous and silent,
A line, invisible, runs through them all.

All the way from Ladoga* you'll trace it.
Right to the Gulf of Finland it does run;
You'll find it on old ordnance maps—those dated
With the dread figures—1941.

Today that line is still alive and breathing,
Knife like, it cuts your very heart in two;
It stirs the forest leaves, like summer breezes;
Where once it ran, stand houses built anew.

Perhaps, today's young generation
Can't see it as will future eyes,
Although in its commemoration
Stone cenotaphs already rise.

Today it still seems to be smoking,
With lightnings flashing through the gloom,
That flaming boundary, where, broken,
The enemy once met his doom.

But hark, they start to speak, the willows!
Come, listen to their rustling speech—
As if the wind, who knew the heroes,
Were calling out the name of each.

Translated by Louis Zellikoff

* Lake near Leningrad, served as the only communication route to the blockaded city.

Перед ночной Арагвой

Был час ночной и поздний,
        Для меня
Желтел фонарь колхозный
        На камнях

Вода плясала
        В свете фонаря,
Моим глазам немало
        Говоря.

Как будто в пенах,
        Вихрях водяных
Мелькали смены
        Быстрых дней моих.

Топя их враз
        В холодной быстрине,
Стальной рассказ
        Река кидала мне.

От строк шумящих
        Глаз отвесть не мог,
От тех летящих
        Леденящих строк.

Их голос плыл
        И в уши грохотал:
«Какой ты был,
        Каким теперь ты стал

Before the Aragva at Night

The hour was late, was lost
in the loud night.
The kolkhoz lantern tossed
its yellowing light

over the stones, the stream
danced quick with gold,
and by that lantern beam
a tale was told,

as if, where spindrift rays
of water clashed,
the wild scenes of my days
flickered and flashed

and drowned, at once, spinning
in chilly race,
a story of steel flung in
my numbing face.

I could not turn, those lines
raved madly past
and rose and froze untwining,
twining fast.

Hoarse in my ears they whirred
a voice was blown:
"Think now of what you were
and what you've grown.

Смотрел в меня,
          В Арагву, ты тогда
При свете дня —
          В те юности года.

Смотри ж сейчас,
          Мы вместе и одни —
В полночный час
          В седой поток взгляни...»

Торчали камни,
          И по их плечам
Стекали славно
          Струи, клокоча.

Я камнем не был,
          Волнами тесним,
И видит небо, —
          Я не буду им.

Фонарь сиял,
          Жестоко обнажив
Зеленый шквал
          И всплески, как ножи.

Сверкали искры
          В свете фонаря,
Как будто освещала их
          Заря.

И каждая жила
          В огне волны,
Как будто шла
          Из самой глубины,

Пронзая ночь
          И ночи непокой...
Я был, Арагва,
          Искрою такой!

"Once on my surges, gay,
you leaned and stared
when all the gold of day
and youth you shared.

"Now we're alone and hush
it's midnight, listen.
See silver-haired they rush
my waves and glisten."

The torrent swirled to drown
in foam the boulders,
a glory of bubbles, down
their streaming shoulders.

But I'm no stone that's drowned
at the wave's will,
and no stone I'll be found,
heaven hear me, still.

The light laid open all
the scalpel'd scene,
the scattering drops, the squall
of furious green.

The lantern strewed about
its spilth of sparks
like dawn that hustles out
the heavy dark

and in the fire of the wave
each lode was rifted
as though from the depths it heaved
glowed and lifted

to pierce the night, pursue
the unresting night.
Aragva, once I too
was leap of light..

Translated by Jack Lindsay

Mirzo Tursun-Zade (b. 1911) is today's leading Tajik poet. He grew up in the village of Karatag which had always been famed for the skill of its craftsmen: potters, tanners and weavers. The poet's father was a craftsman too. Mirzo means "scribe", a name which was given only to those who could read and write and was therefore a title of honour. Tursun-Zade was educated at the first Soviet boarding school to be established by the state, and then at Tashkent University. He has loved poetry since his childhood, and his first teachers, he says, were Rudaki, Hafiz and Bedil. He was one of the first to incorporate modern themes and rhythms into the traditional patterns of Eastern poetry.

Most of his themes are connected with the East, and his most important works are "Indian Ballad", "The Gissar Valley" and "Hassan-Arbakesh". Mirzo Tursun-Zade is a prominent public figure, and 1960 Lenin Prize winner.

MIRZO TURSUN-ZADE

МИРЗО ТУРСУН-ЗАДЕ

Сестра моя Африка

Кто не слышал об Африке гневной, о песне большой
О невольнице смуглой с красивой и смелой душой?
Кто не знает об Африке — черной, далекой стране,
Что пылала в огне от широких дорог в стороне?

Кто не помнит, как плыли к ее берегам корабли
За товаром живым, за сокровищем чудной земли?

Благородную землю, чье тело чернее чернил,
Вероломств и насилья кровавый поток обагрил.

Белолицые хищники мучили тело ее,
В черной Африке делали черное дело свое.

Шли года, шли века — под бичом чужеземца-врага
Та земля превратилась в рабыню, в чьем ухе серьга,
И мятежные слезы, алмазные слезы лила
Там, где копи алмазные, там, где древесная мгла...

О сестра, под луной ты мне виделась издалека,
Вкруг луны ореолом — рыдающие облака.
Против скал угнетения, против твердынь палача.
Океан Атлантический волны катил, клокоча.
Крик о помощи, крик, обращенный к своим и чужим

My Sister, Africa!

Who has not heard of Africa, beautiful, noble and brave,
Of the ebon-skinned beauty held fast in the chains of a
slave,
Of the sufferings borne by the victim of famine and
strife,
Torn and tortured, afar from the highways of life,

Of the ships that put off for the palm-circled harbours
in quest
Of live prey, from the shores of the cannibal West,

Of the fabulous land, of the body as black as the night
Red with blood at the hands of the villainous white.

Limb from limb she was rent by the pale-featured mob;
In the heart of black Africa's jungles they did their
black job.

Years and centuries passed, foreign beasts marking time
with their whip,
Turning Africa into a slave with a ring in her lip.
With hot tears, tears of wrath, tears like diamonds did
Africa weep
In the heart of the jungles, in diamond mines gloomy and
deep.

O my sister, how clearly I pictured you, far to the
South,
With an agonised death-cry distorting your sensitive
mouth,
With the horrified moon shrinking back in the clouds at
the sight
Of her chain-bound beloved tormented by day and by night.
Filled with wrath at those murderous deeds, the sea
rolled its waves;

487

Исторгался из сердца Сахары, как огненный дым.
И, в неволе сгорая, мечтали арабы, чтоб Нил
Жажду, жажду свободы прохладной струей утолил!

Был от мира сокрыт материк за тюремной стеной,
Но живых африканцев у нас мы встречали весной.
Прилетали из Африки птицы и в свежем тепле
Для себя находили жилища у нас на земле,
И, на время забыв о свирепых ловцах, о силках,
Долгожданной свободой дышали у нас в цветниках.
Возвращались назад — мы просили пернатых послов
Передать африканцам от нас много дружеских слов...

Шли года, шли века — и другие пришли времена.
Между миром и Африкой рушится рабства стена!
Между миром и Африкой стали короче пути:
Ведь свобода идет по земле, дни и ночи в пути!
Сторона чужедальняя стала нам ближе, чем встарь,
Стал яснее для нас языков африканских словарь.
Кровь борца никогда от людских не сокроется глаз,
В каждой капельке крови бурлящей свобода зажглась!

Начинается в мире иная, иная пора,
Поднимается Африка — наша родная сестра.
Не глухой, заколдованный лес, не пустыня она,
Посмотри: не рабыня она — героиня она!
Ей могилу копали, чтоб солнце низринулось в ночь,
Но она прогоняет последних могильщиков прочь.
И в лесах, и в саваннах, и возле седых пирамид,
За свободу борясь, о свободе она говорит.

Ты спроси: кто работает, к братьям любви не тая?
И Каир выступает вперед: «Это я, это я!»
Кто решил, чтобы сделались вольными предков края?
И Алжир непреклонный встает: «Это я, это я!»
Кто впервые хозяйкою стала родного жилья?
Слышим Аккру с далеких широт: «Это я, это я!»
Кто народу отрадней, милее, чем амбры струя?
Конакри издалёка поёт: «Это я, это я!»
Кто взывает в бою: «Помоги мне, о братьев семья!»?
Говорит конголезский народ: «Это я, это я!»
Кто же саван для недруга шьет, — нет нужнее шитья?
Океан свое слово берет: «Это я, это я!»

O how often it drowned in its depths the despair of
your slaves!
Calling loudly for rescue, appealing to known and
unknown,
From the heart of the burning Sahara came groan after
groan.
Pining under their yoke, longed the Arabs to slake from
the Nile
Their unbearable thirst—thirst for freedom from
conquerors vile.

Iron walls shut the continent off from the rest of the
world,
Iron walls of the jail into which her proud nations were
hurled.
Yet we welcomed live Africans here in the Spring—
They were Africa's messengers—birds on the wing.
In the shade of our gardens through summer they
nested,
In the land of the free from oppression they rested.
When they started back home, feathered envoys, we asked
them to tell
What we felt for the Africans groaning in day-to-day
hell.

Years and centuries passed—till at last other days
have arrived,
Now are Africa's hopes for delivery being revived!
Walls are falling that barred her before from the
world,
Soon, aye, soon from her shoulders the yoke will be
hurled!
For the glorious Spirit of Freedom is well on its way.
Better known to us all is the Africa of today
For indeed, all the world has now entered upon a new
life.
She arises—our sister, the land where oppression ran
rife;
Bound for freedom, for freedom she struggles and raises
her voice,
And with her, and for her all the world's other nations
rejoice.

А в ответ восклицают моря, города и поля —
Это с Африкой, кажется мне, говорит вся земля:

«Слышу, Африка, слышу тебя, дорогая сестра,
Мы с тобою пойдем по дороге любви и добра,
И, достигнув свободы, постигнув расцвет бытия,
Скажешь братьям-народам: «Друзья, это я, это я!

Cheers for Africa's freedom re-echo through nations and
lands
To new Africa gladly extending in friendship their hands.

Translated by Dorian Rottenberg

Vladimir Tsybin (b. 1932) is a descendant of Russian Cossacks who emigrated to Asia. His home was the steppe-land, encircled with· snow-capped mountains. The traditions of freedom-loving Cossacks with their cult of physical strength and their enormous vitality find an interesting reflection in Tsybin's poetry. It is earthy and vivid in imagery, the comparisons are richly sensuous, and the language is colourful and dynamic. Tsybin's most recent books are "Pulse" and "Insomnia of the Age" (both 1963).

VLADIMIR TSYBIN

ВЛАДИМИР ЦЫБИН

Праздники

Юрию Казакову

Сны на подушке —
как пчелы на песке...
Сны мне сулили:
праздники,
праздники.
Праздники!
Они приходили
в гулких весенних капелях,
с крутящимся смехом
на бешеных каруселях,
с качелями,
с ярмарками,
с яствами на столах
и с тульскими пряниками
в руках!

Начинал я мать просить:
— В изголовье мне посыпь
ты не льна, не зерна,
а про праздники сна!

И виделось явственно
ночами мне лютыми:
праздники уходили
медленными верблюдами...
И я им кричал:
— Вернитесь! —

Holidays

To Yuri Kazakov

Like bees in a beehive,
my dreams when I slumber.
They promised me holidays,
gay,
without number.
Holidays!
They came with the ring
of the spring's merry laughter,
with gay, festive crowds,
and the kids skipping after,
with games
and with goodies
heaped high on the tables:
candies and boxes
with beautiful labels.

Mother I'd beg:
"Put no food at my head,
no cookies, nor creams,
but some beautiful dreams!"

And saw I most clearly
on nights, wild and dreary,
the holidays receding,
like caravans weary....
And I would shout after:
"Come back!"

И просыпался,
и спрашивал маму:
— Куда мой праздник девался?

Сны на подушке —
как пчелы на пасеке...
— Где твои праздники?
На войне твои праздники...

И сохло утро
посредине белого неба,
где не звезды,
а крошки военного хлеба.
Приходили беженцы к маме,
и скучали

        беженцы горько,
и просили праздника —
а была того праздника
корка,
черствая корка!
О, эти корочки горькие...
Но жили праздники,
спрятанные в треугольники,
их присылала маме
и нам

        полевая почта...
И мне, как на качелях,
было страшно

        и просто.
Праздники!
Праздники!
Мы без праздников все вырастали
Наши праздники полегли
под звездами

        и крестами,
возвращались праздники
на костылях
и слепые.
От этих праздников
становились мамы — седые...
— Эх, пехота, пехота!
Полегла ты у дальней высотки...

Then awaken,
and mother I'd ask
who my holiday'd taken.

Like bees in a beehive,
my dreams when I'm sleeping...
"Now where are your holidays?"
At the war they are keeping....

And in the pale heaven
the morning was fading,
with stars,
like breadcrumbs of wartime parading.
Sad refugees came to my mother,
with anguish
                    behind them,

and begged for a holiday,
but its crust
was all she could find them.
Dry crust!
Oh, those crusts, so sweet, and so bitter
But holidays came
in each brief soldiers' letter.
They came to my mother—
by field post
                    delivered.
And I, feeling heady,
delighted
          and shivered.
Oh, holidays!
Holidays!
Our childhood losses,
Our holidays fell
'neath the stars
and the crosses.

And back came the holidays,
blinded
          and crippled.
The heads of our mothers
with grey hairs they stippled.
"Oh, soldiers! oh, soldiers!

Молодела роса,
и земля гнала в завязи соки.

...И верил я в праздники
и ждал их —
вернутся верблюды
и вернут на горбах своих
давнее горькое чудо,
ибо то, чему веришь,
исполнится в сроки
                                    разные,
ибо надо же верить!
Особенно веровать
                                    в праздники!
Верьте в праздники,
как в теплые запахи
                                    леса!..
Я и сам привожу их
матери
            на все лето.

'Neath the sod you were lying..."
And the earth was in bloom,
and the winds gently sighing.

I believed in the holidays,
and I eagerly waited:
they'd return
like the caravans,
bringing gifts,
though belated,
for things will come true,
if you trust ever freshly,
so always believe!
and in holidays,
                    specially!
Believe,
as in woodland delights,
                    without number!
I bring them myself
to my mother
                    each summer.

Translated by Eugene Felgenhauer

Simon Chikovani (1903-1966), an outstanding Georgian poet, was born in a mountain village on the Black Sea coast. "The breath of the sea reached the poplars in our garden.... Tall mountains, smothered in a purplish mist, surrounded our village on three sides. At first I could not distinguish the distant mountains from the clouds." In romantic Svanetia, the highest part of Georgia where medieval towers stand gazing into bottomless chasms, Chikovani listened to ancient legends and took them down in writing. He travelled a great deal, his wanderlust remaining as strong in his later days as it was in his youth. He has written many poems about the Ukraine, Armenia and Russia. The image of the road is to be found throughout his work. Chikovani's lyricism is distinguished by its subtle psychology, its dignity, and the great expressiveness of its imagery. His most widely known poem is the "Song of David Guramishvili". Simon Chikovani has also made superb translations of the "Lay of Igor's Host" and Taras Shevchenko's lyrical poems into Georgian.

SIMON CHIKOVANI

СИМОН ЧИКОВАНИ

На сенокосе

Как пьяно пахнет это сено!
В его росе твои колена.
Иди ко мне!
Скорей иди!
Забудь все прошлое мгновенно.
Меня не думать убеди.
И сладостно и откровенно
В цветы и сено упади!

Швырни пахучей горстью тута,
глазами темными маня.
С тобой не будет мне уюта.
Ты как восстание,
как смута.
Ты моя сладкая минута
и вечность горькая моя!

Меня и засухой пытало,
меня и голодом шатало,
но снисхожденья не прошу.
И раз пора косить настала,
мне быть усталым не пристало!
Ты погляди, как я кошу!

Стирая добрый пот обильный,
я, молодой,
                    большой и сильный.
свою косу точу не зря.
Так помоги, брусок точильный,
чтобы горела,
как заря!

Haymaking

It's mowing time; I'll whet my scythe
With dawn's first golden ray and dew;
Come out to me, beloved Life
I'll spread the fragrant hay for you.

Come, Life, to me—new deeds I'll dare,
Your harvest rich around me spread,
Your dreams and sorrows let me share
As on your breast I rest my head.

I've thirsted with the sun-parched
                                soil,
Converted wastes to gardens fair;
Now in my Autumn, from my toil,
With singing heart I home repair.

With cherished dreams I'll whet my
                                scythe
Until its blade outshines the sun.
Come out to me, beloved Life,
Caress me as you would your son.

But should I slumber, raise your voice
And from my eyes drive sleep away.
So, ripe in years, I may rejoice
In you as in my early day.

Любимая,
навстречу вышли
к тебе и яблони и вишни,
и просьба всей моей души
как гроздь,
ты сердце мое выжми,
потом еще немного выжди
и, запрокинув,
осуши!

Wring out my heart, until its drops
Bedew fair Georgia's hills and plains,
And from her snow-capped mountain tops
Reflect the glory of my plains.

Translated by Louis Zellikoff

Стихи начать — как жизнь построить

                        снова

и не могу я разгадать черед
живых приливов и отливов слова,
хоть душу мне зародыш песни жжет.

Что стоит стих, с которым из гортани
душа не хлынет? На его призыв
не отзовется горных вод журчанье,
цветок не вздрогнет, венчик приоткрыв.

Скажи мне, песня, что твоя основа?
Отрада ближних, боль от ран моих,
дождь — воспитатель хлеба золотого,
или туман в морщинах гор седых?

Рябь на воде? Плоты на синей глади?
Дыханье сена, сметанного в стог?
Иль у моей единственной во взгляде
за огоньком бегущий огонек?

Начать стихи не легче, чем сомненья
стереть, — сплошную ржавчину с души,
в кустах найти кольцо, в одно мгновенье
звезду избрать (все в небе хороши).

The Birth of Song

The birth of song is fraught with joy and sorrow,
Like building life anew—one endless quest;
Today I know not what I'll write tomorrow
Though ere its birth my song gnaws at my breast.

That song is mute though from the throat it gushes,
Which from the heart and soul doth fail to spring,
To which no streamlet sings, no blossom blushes—
It is no song, whoever it may sing.

So tell me song—what is it gives you birth?
Another's joy? The pain that burns my breast?
The showers of spring that saturate the earth?
Or mists that on the hoary mountains rest?

And tell me song, whence does your music rise?
From ripples on the lake? rafts river-borne?
The fire of my beloved's sparkling eyes?
The fragrance of the new-mown hay at dawn?

The birth of song is fraught with tribulation,
Like fighting doubt that eats your heart away,
Like choosing stars from out a constellation,
Or looking for a needle in the hay.

Нет во вселенной силы непреклонней
мечты, взращенной сердца глубиной.
Стих — это ладан тлеет на ладони,
стих — это юность спорит с сединой.

The dream that from the heart of hearts emerges,
No power in heaven or earth can ever slay;
For song is fragrant incense ever burning,
It is the "Yea" of Youth 'gainst Age's "Nay".

Translated by Louis Zellikoff

Stepan Shchipachev (b. 1889) is one of the most popular poets of the older generation. He has a distinct identity and a place of his own in Russian poetry as a master of thumbnail stories in verse with a moral to each one of them. His style is aphoristic, and the form he often uses is that of a laconic parable. More than one generation of young people have learnt his "Lines of Love" by heart. In recent years Shchipachev has devoted much time and effort to the training of young poets. He continues to experiment with new rhythms and rhymes, as will be seen from his collections "Musings" (1962), "A Man's Hand" (1964), and "Selected Works" in Two Volumes (1965).

STEPAN SHCHIPACHEV

СТЕПАН ЩИПАЧЕВ

Ладонь
большая мужская.
Её —
отчетливы и грубы —
линии пересекают,
дороги твоей судьбы.

Она
от кирки и лопаты грубела,
на женской груди робела.

Ладонь — это жизни слепок,
годов пролетевших следы.
В нее запрокинется небо,
когда зачерпнешь воды.

Она широка, пятипала.
Плывешь — рассекает реку.
В армейском строю прикипала
Под знаменем красным
к древку.

Она —
чтобы гладить ребенка
с любовью, тревогой отца...
И чтобы пощечиной звонкой
обжечь подлеца.

The Palm of a Man's Hand

The palm of a man's hand,
                                        broad in span
Big and strong,
                        a manly hand.
Crossed with deep-cut, ridged lines,
The roads he will travel,
                                        clearly defined.
It's hard when a lever it presses,
Shy when a breast it caresses.

The palm is a cast of man's career,
A record of what he has done.
Scoop up some water, and you will see
The sky in there, overturned.

It takes you across to the other bank,
An oar without a snag.
Remember when you were in the ranks.
How firmly it gripped the flag?

Your palm is there to gently stroke
The baby on your lap,
And give a scoundrel, when provoked,
A ringing, smarting slap.

Округлое, как планета,
покоится яблоко в ней.
Пускай же ладони этой
не будет на свете честней!

Your palm holds an apple so snugly
As if it were cradling the earth.
So let it stay clean and unsullied,
Let honesty measure its worth.

Translated by Olga Shartse

Мы трудимся, над строчками не ленимся
и никого не надо торопить.
Растет, растет стихов поленица,
которыми и печь не растопить.
Чадят, шипят... А может, зря сурово
сужу об этом? Все мечту таим,
что кто-то, кто-то, словно атом, слово
вдруг расщепит и мир согреет им.

We're working hard, we're writing veritable screeds,
To push us on or ask for more there is no need.
The stack of poems grows forever higher,
Too damp and raw to even start a fire.
They hiss and smoke.... But maybe that's too strong.
I shouldn't judge them so. For in our hearts we long
That one of us will like the atom split the word
And it will suddenly give warmth to all the world.

Translated by Olga Shartse

Прощание с зимой

Деревья в снегу, и в снегу дома.
Недели идут за неделями.
Мне грустно прощаться с тобою, зима
с морозами и метелями.

Стояла, до ряби в глазах бела,
явив красоту свою пышную,
и в той красоте
не один замела
след жизни, как тропку лыжную.

Быть может, и я навсегда с такой
прощаюсь под звездами белыми.
Я снег твой до хруста сжимаю рукой,
не знаю, зачем это делаю.

Farewell to Winter

The trees clad in snow, and the houses too.
But week follows week and it's turning warm.
I'm sorry to say goodbye to you,
I'll miss you, your frosts and snows and storms.

You dazzled the eyes, you were so white,
And lost in that beauty magnificent
Were traces of many a life, wiped out
As if they were ski-tracks made recently.

Beneath the white stars for the last time I stand,
I never may see you like this again.
A lump of your snow I crush in my hand,
But why do I do it, I couldn't explain....

Translated by Olga Shartse

Не верю!

Человечество — это река.
В воображении передо мной
проходят века —
волна за волной, волна за волной
Звенят и плещутся говоры стран.
Пускай далек еще тот океан,
в который катится эта река.
Не верю!
Не может такая река
вдруг оборваться, как эта строка.

Mankind to me is a river of nations
The ages, I see in imagination,
As waves rolling on towards the sea,
Wave upon wave, mighty and free,
Splashing and ringing in different tongues.
The way to the sea may still be long,
But the river is rolling, it's rolling along,
And I'll never believe that a current so strong
Could break off as suddenly as my poor song.

Translated by Olga Shartse

Ilya Ehrenburg (1891-1967) was a celebrated publicist and author of novels and books on art. As a poet he was less popular, yet his book "Poetry 1938-1958" (1959) was sold out within an hour. In poetry as in prose Ehrenburg was a penetrating historian, but while in his novels and articles he recorded the passage of time in constant motion, in a stream of facts, faces and events, in his poetry he brought out the substance of life, the very essence of spiritual processes. "Spanish Poems", "Paris 1940", "May 9, 1945" and the titles of his other collections of verse are in themselves a chronicle of this century's main events. Ehrenburg's poetry reflects the soul of a man of the 20th century with its torments, impulses and hope.

ILYA EHRENBURG

ИЛЬЯ ЭРЕНБУРГ

Да разве могут дети юга,
Где розы плещут в декабре,
Где не разыщешь слова «вьюга»
Ни в памяти, ни в словаре,
Да разве там, где небо сине
И не слиняет ни на час,
Где испокон веков поныне
Все то же лето тешит глаз,
Да разве им хоть так, хоть вкратце
Хоть на минуту, хоть во сне,
Хоть ненароком догадаться,
Что значит думать о весне,
Что значит в мартовские стужи,
Когда отчаянье берет,
Все ждать и ждать, как неуклюже
Зашевелится грузный лед.
А мы такие зимы знали,
Вжились в такие холода,
Что даже не было печали,
Но только гордость и беда.
И в крепкой, ледяной обиде,
Сухой пургой ослеплены,
Мы видели, уже не видя,
Глаза зеленые весны.

How can the folk in tropics dwelling,
Where roses in December grow,
Where people hardly know the spelling
Of words like "blizzard" and "ice floe",
Where ever azure, ever pleasant,
Above them sails a silken sky,
Since time primordial to the present,
The selfsame summer soothes the eye.
How can they even for a twinkling,
In slumber, or in daydream learn,
How can they have the slightest inkling
Of what it means for spring to yearn,
Or how in freezing winter vainly,
When dour despondency holds sway,
To wait and wait until ungainly
And massive ice gets under way.
But we have known such wintry madness,
Have learned such coldness to abide,
No longer have we room for sadness
But only misery and pride.
With cold resentment in our being,
When blizzards blinded everything,
We pictured, without really seeing,
The halcyon days of verdant spring.

Translated by Eugene Felgenhauer

Сердце солдата

Бухгалтер он, счетов охапка,
Семерки, тройки п нули.
И кажется, он спит, как папка
В тяжелой голубой пыли.
Но вот он с другом повстречался.
Ни цифр, ни сплетен, ни котлет.
Уж нет его, пропал бухгалтер,
Он весь в огне прошедших лет.
Как дробь, стучит солдата сердце:
«До Петушков рукой подать!»
Беги! Рукой подать до смерти,
А жизнь в одном — перебежать.
Ты скажешь — это от контузий,
Пройдет, найдет он жизни нить,
Но нити спутались, и узел
Уж не распутать — разрубить.

Друзья и сверстники развалин
И строек сверстники, мой край,
Мы сорок лет не разувались,
И если нам приснится рай,
Мы не поверим.
            Стой, не мешкай,
Не для того мы здесь, чтоб спать!
Какой там рай? Есть перебежка —
До Петушков рукой подать!

The Heart of a Soldier

All day he's sitting and ledgers keeping,
With tens and sevens he conjure must.
At times it seems that he is sleeping
Among the heavy and bluish dust.
But now a comrade he has encountered.
Away all figures and gossip fly.
He is no longer an accountant,
He's all aflame with years gone by.
Tatoo the soldier's heart is beating:
"It's half a mile to Petushki!"
Run on! There can be no retreating,
One aim—to rout the enemy.
You say the reason's severe contusion,
It'll pass, he'll find the thread of life;
Alas, the threads are in such confusion,
They'll not unravel, they need a knife.
We are coevals and friends of ruins,
Of great constructions coevals we,
For forty years we've kept our shoes on,
And if in dreams we heaven see,
We'll not believe.

        Hey there, don't tarry!
It's not for sleeping that here we be!
What good is heaven? We have to hurry—
It's half a mile to Petushki!

Translated by Eugene Felgenhauer

Alexander Yashin (1913-1968) was born and raised in a village in northern Russia where the forests are dense and endless, and where the purity of the local language, ancient superstitions, customs and dress have been preserved to this day. In the 1940s Yashin's poetry was very colourful in its language, but in subject matter it was superficial and fell far short of life's serious demands. However his talent matured, and the last ten or fifteen years have made him one of the best-known of our poets with a deep sense of civic responsibility and a significant message to his readers. Such is his book "Integrity" (1961). He sets high moral standards and demands integrity and an honest attitude to life. Lately Alexander Yashin has also made a successful debut as a prose writer.

ALEXANDER YASHIN

АЛЕКСАНДР ЯШИН

В несметном нашем богатстве
Слова драгоценные есть:
  Отечество,
  Верность,
  Братство.
А есть еще:
  Совесть,
  Честь...
Ах, если бы все понимали,
Что это не просто слова,
Каких бы мы бед избежали.
И это не просто слова!

When we speak of the things that we treasure,
That we prize above all, we include
      words like MOTHERLAND,
            LOYALTY,
            HONOUR,
    words like FRIENDSHIP
        and
        BROTHERHOOD.
No, these words aren't just words, empty words.
And if only to all this were plain,
Much that plagues us today could we banish,
Much of sorrow would go, and of pain.
Nor are these only words, empty words!

Translated by Irina Zheleznova

Добрые дела

Мне с отчимом невесело жилось,
Все ж он меня растил —
И оттого
Порой жалею, что не довелось
Хоть чем-нибудь порадовать его.

Когда он слег и тихо умирал, —
Рассказывает мать, —
День ото дня
Все чаще вспоминал меня и ждал:
«Вот Шурку бы... Уж он бы спас меня!»

Бездомной бабушке в селе родном
Я говорил: мол, так ее люблю,
Что подрасту и сам срублю ей дом,
Дров наготовлю,
Хлеба воз куплю.

Мечтал о многом,
Много обещал...
В блокаде ленинградской старика
От смерти б спас,
Да на день опоздал,
И дня того не возвратят века.

Теперь прошел я тысячи дорог —
Купить воз хлеба, дом срубить бы мог...
Нет отчима,
И бабка умерла...

Спешите делать добрые дела!

Kind Deeds

I was his stepson, not his son, and yet,
Though things were none too easy, I regret
That never was I truly kind or good
To him who brought me up from babyhood.

When, at the end, he lay awaiting death
He asked for me, and with his dying breath,
My mother tells me,
Whispered, "If he came,
If he but came, I would be well again!..."

I liked a poor old lady once, and said
I'd buy her bags of sweets and sacks
                                    of bread,
And stack her shed with wood when I was grown,
And build a house,
A house for her alone.

Rash promises...
I made them by the score!
The Leningrad blockade,
An open door....
I asked a sick and hungry man to wait,
I said I'd come,
                and did—
A day too late!

A thousand roads,
A thousand have I trod....
Now I could build that house
And buy that bread.
But they are gone who once my help did need.
Make haste!
Do not postpone a kindly deed!

Translated by Irina Zheleznova

www.ingramcontent.com/pod-product-compliance
Lightning Source LLC
Chambersburg PA
CBHW010043090426
42734CB00017B/3229